GUIDE TO AMERICA–HOLY LAND STUDIES
1620–1948

AMERICA–HOLY LAND STUDIES

Project Director and General Editor	Moshe Davis
Co-Directors	Selig Adler Robert T. Handy
Editorial Coordinators	Nathan M. Kaganoff, U.S.A. Menahem Kaufman, Israel

A Joint Project of the
American Jewish Historical Society
Ruth B. Fein, President
Lloyd H. Klatzkin, Chairman of the American
Jewish Historical Society-Institute of
Contemporary Jewry Liaison Committee
Bernard Wax, Director, American Jewish Historical Society
and the
Institute of Contemporary Jewry
The Hebrew University of Jerusalem
Daniel G. Ross, Chairman of the Institute's
International Planning Committee
Mordechai Altshuler, Head, Institute of Contemporary Jewry
Yehuda Bauer, Academic Chairman,
International Planning Committee
Lucy D. Manoff, Coordinator, U.S.A.

GUIDE TO AMERICA–HOLY LAND STUDIES
1620–1948
Volume 3

Economic Relations and Philanthropy

Edited by
Nathan M. Kaganoff

Introduction by
Moshe Davis

PRAEGER SPECIAL STUDIES • PRAEGER SCIENTIFIC

New York • Philadelphia • Eastbourne, UK
Toronto • Hong Kong • Tokyo • Sydney

Library of Congress Cataloging in Publication Data

Main entry under title:

Guide to America–Holy Land Studies, 1620–1948.

Includes index.
Contents: —v.3. Economic Relations
and Philanthropy.
1. Palestine—Library resources.   2. United States—
Relations—Palestine—Library resources   3. Palestine—
Relations—United States—Library resources.
I. Kaganoff, Nathan M.
Z3476.G84   1983   016.95694   82-13322
ISBN 0-03-064244-2

Ongoing research is supported by
the Jacob Blaustein Fund for American Studies

Published in 1983 by Praeger Publishers
CBS Educational and Professional Publishing
a Division of CBS Inc.
521 Fifth Avenue, New York, NY 10175 USA

©1983 by Praeger Publishers

3456789   052   987654321

Printed in the United States of America
on acid-free paper

With devotion to
Milton J. Krensky
for his everlasting contribution to
America and the Holy Land

PREFACE

We are pleased to present to the academic community Volume 3 of the *Guide to America-Holy Land Studies 1620-1948*, which contains material on economic relations and philanthropy.

The origin of the project that has brought about the publication of this series of volumes and the manner in which the material was assembled has been described in both Volumes 1 and 2. The reader is referred to the Preface of either volume for this information.

In all three volumes of the *Guide*, the descriptions are specifically intended to uncover potential sources of new information. We decided very early in our planning to conduct a long-range institution-by-institution search with detailed, objective descriptions of material relevant to our subject rather than concentrate on collections that have already been utilized by scholars. We thought this method would be most immediately beneficial to the cause of scholarship. Clearly, a project of this magnitude ought not wait for publication until all the surveys are completed. Such an endeavor could conceivably take a generation. Hence, we decided to publish the information currently at our disposal as the project continues. In essence, since we began our work we realized that we had virtually uncovered a new and exciting field of research, larger than we had originally anticipated. In the course of time, as the volumes appear based on thematic organization, the full picture will evolve and a comprehensive organization can then be undertaken.

Since we are providing scholars with descriptions of numerous collections that were previously unlisted and most of them never before used, we intentionally refrain from making value judgements on the various collections. All of the archives and libraries we select house material of historic value, allowing scholars to determine which sources are relevant to their own research. Indeed, what is a primary need for one scholar may be a secondary need for another.

The present volume contains descriptions of manuscript and archival collections that relate to economic contacts and philanthropic efforts between America and the Holy Land. Each description is followed by the initials of the researcher who examined the collection and prepared the data; the numbers indicate the month and the year when the material was examined. When contacting a repository, it would be advisable to indicate the date of the description since the holdings of many libraries undergo major changes in cataloging or arrangement with the passage of time.

Obviously, our researchers are completely dependent on the staff or the catalog of the institutions they visit to direct them to collections containing appropriate material. If there are corrections or modifications to be made in matters of detail, please bring them to our attention. Moreover, if any of our readers know of additional collections, we would appreciate being informed of their existence, as we plan to publish a list of corrigenda in future volumes.

The number of repositories containing collections is quite large. In editing the material, particularly of the first section, we were rather surprised at the quantity of collections containing information on efforts by individuals in the United States to develop economic contact with the Holy Land. Popular belief has always maintained that this area of the Turkish Empire was "an economic wasteland." While it is true that many of the efforts reflect Zionist interest in developing a viable economy for the Holy Land, it was still unexpected to have discovered the large number of attempts made by American businessmen to accomplish similar goals.

The second portion of the volume is devoted to charitable activity by Americans on behalf of people in this region. Here also the results were unexpected. We have always been led to believe that the beneficence of people throughout the world was what sustained the residents of the Holy Land. From our research and material we have already culled, it would seem to be more accurate to conclude that, certainly in the nineteenth century, Jews in the Holy Land sought self-sufficiency and for the most part provided for their own needs.

Once again it is my pleasant duty to acknowledge the guidance of Dr. Moshe Davis. One cannot exaggerate the difficulties faced in coordinating work that has been produced in several parts of the world. Special thanks go to Mr. Yohai Goell, Mrs. Ora Zimmer, Mrs. Lottie K. Davis, and Mr. Bernard Wax, Director of the American Jewish Historical Society, who reviewed the manuscript line by line through its various drafts. Dr. Selig Adler and Dr. Robert T. Handy provided the editor with numerous valuable suggestions and helpful insights. Dr. Menahem Kaufman, my counterpart in Israel, and Mira Levine have compiled and edited the Israeli material gathered during 1981-1982 and included in this volume. We extend our appreciation as well to Ms. Lucy Manoff, Institute Coordinator in the United States, and Ms. Roni Kleinman who so ably supervise and administer the America-Holy Land Project and this *Guide* series.

The first and second volumes were received enthusiastically. We trust that the present volume will evoke a similar reaction.

Waltham, Massachusetts   Nathan M. Kaganoff
January, 1983

LIST OF RESEARCHERS

The names of the researchers, responsible for the accompanying descriptions, and whose initials follow each item, are:

Rosalind Arzt
Samuel Ashbel
Ron Bartour
Tzionah Bin-Nun
Elanah Ehrlich
Adina Feldstern
Marvin Feuerwerger
David Frost
Sylvan Ginsburgh
Yohai Goell
Tsafrit Greenberg
Sophie Haber
Simone Kessler
Hannah Koevary
Mira Levine
Ralph Melnick
Deborah Price
Danby Ring
Jonathan D. Sarna
Shifra Shor
Jeanne Talpers
Ora Zimmer

LIST OF REPOSITORIES

AMERICAN JEWISH ARCHIVES, Clifton Avenue, Cincinnati, Ohio 45220, U.S.A.

AMERICAN JEWISH HISTORICAL SOCIETY LIBRARY, 2 Thornton Road, Waltham, Massachusetts 02154, U.S.A.

ARCHAEOLOGICAL (ROCKEFELLER) MUSEUM, MINISTRY OF
    EDUCATION AND CULTURE, DEPARTMENT OF
    ANTIQUITIES, P.O. Box 586, Jerusalem, Israel

ARCHDIOCESE OF BOSTON ARCHIVES, 2121 Commonwealth
    Avenue, Brighton, Massachusetts 02135, U.S.A.

CENTRAL ZIONIST ARCHIVES, King George Avenue, Jerusalem
    (mailing address: P.O. Box 92, Jerusalem 91000, Israel)

COLUMBIA UNIVERSITY LIBRARY, New York, New York
    10027, U.S.A.

FRIENDS UNITED MEETING, Wider Ministries Commission,
    101 Quaker Hill Drive, Richmond, Indiana 47374, U.S.A.

HADASSAH, 50 West 58th Street, New York, New York 10019,
    U.S.A.

HAKIBBUTZ HAMEUHAD, Yad Tabenkin, Ramat Gan, Israel

HOUGHTON LIBRARY, Harvard University, Cambridge,
    Massachusetts 02138, U.S.A.

ISRAEL STATE ARCHIVES, Prime Minister's Office, Qiryat
    Ben-Gurion, Building 3, Jerusalem, Israel

ISRAEL FILM ARCHIVES, Jerusalem Cinematheque, Wolfson
    Garden, Hevron Road, Jerusalem (mailing address: P.O. Box
    4455, Jerusalem 91043, Israel)

JABOTINSKY INSTITUTE IN ISRAEL, 38 King George Street,
    Tel Aviv, Israel

JERUSALEM MUNICIPALITY–HISTORICAL ARCHIVES,
    Talpioth, Efrata Road 20, Jerusalem, Israel

JEWISH NATIONAL AND UNIVERSITY LIBRARY, Givat Ram Campus, P.O. Box 503, Jerusalem, Israel

PUBLIC RECORD OFFICE, Portugal Street, London WC1, England

STERLING MEMORIAL LIBRARY, Yale University, New Haven, Connecticut 06520, U.S.A.

THE TEMPLE, University Circle and Silver Park, Cleveland, Ohio 44106, U.S.A.

UNITED STATES NATIONAL ARCHIVES AND RECORDS SERVICE, Washington, D.C. 20408, U.S.A.

YAD YITZHAK BEN ZVI, 17 Ibn Gabirol Street, Jerusalem 92430, Israel

YIVO INSTITUTE FOR JEWISH RESEARCH, Fifth Avenue and 86th Street, New York, New York 10028, U.S.A.

ZIONIST ARCHIVES AND LIBRARY, 515 Park Avenue, New York, New York 10022, U.S.A.

INTRODUCTION

The present volume of the *Guide* follows bibliographic procedures introduced in Volume 1, *American Presence*, and Volume 2, *Political Relations and American Zionism*. While the selected themes suggest methodological compartmentalization, annotated references in all three volumes reveal substantive interconnections. As students of this series have already discovered, vital historical information is often tucked away in unsuspected corners and appended notes. Also, significant evaluative material is interspersed throughout the collections.

Striking examples of such interspersion in this volume, *Economic Relations and Philanthropy*, are three documents from separate repositories written within the space of thirteen months (January 1944-February 1945). All three sources deal with economic projects that are at the same time politically directed, with concrete reference to American concerns. The first (listed under Great Britain Foreign Office), researched in the Public Record Office, London, is a letter (dated January 17, 1944) from W. G. Hayter of the British Embassy in Washington. Essentially, it introduces the first publication of the American Institute, which "outlines the scheme of a systematic programme of research into the economic potentialities of Palestine."

The second item (listed under Atkins, Paul), culled from the Historical Manuscripts in the Sterling Memorial Library at Yale University in New Haven, Connecticut, is a 22-page report entitled "Conditions in Syria, Lebanon, Palestine, Egypt, Trans-Jordan, Iraq and Arabia" by Paul M. Atkins, Consulting Economist. This report is based on observations made during a trip of about three weeks duration in January, 1944. At that time Mr. Atkins was returning from a year in Iran where he had served as economic advisor to the Imperial Government.

The third item (dated February 17, 1945), jointly signed by naval and army officers, is found in the Records of the Office of Strategic Services R & A (Research and Analysis) Confidential Reports. Prepared by the J.I.C.A. (Joint Intelligence Collection

Agency) in Cairo, Egypt, the memorandum is marked "Palestine–
Hayes' Plan for the Irregation [sic] of Palestine."

How do these references correlate American economic, political
and domestic interests? The following citations illustrate:

From the W. G. Hayter Report:

> . . . The [American Palestine] Institute was formed by persons who
> believe that the economic possibilities of Palestine are greater than
> His Majesty's Government has ever conceded them to be, and that if
> they were seriously examined by persons unaffected by the non-
> economic considerations militating against the Zionist programme in
> Palestine, facts would emerge pointing to immigration possibilities
> at present denied by British experts. . . .
>
> . . . This material should not be dismissed as routine Zionist
> propaganda, since it issues from persons likely to be regarded with
> considerable respect (particularly by the White House so long as the
> present incumbent remains there) as experts at least as competent
> to advise on these topics as anyone whom the Near Eastern Division
> of the State Department or the Foreign Economic Administration
> is able to produce.

From the Paul Atkins Conclusion:

> . . . The opportunities open to American petroleum companies in the
> Near East are very great, but they involve serious problems with far-
> reaching diplomatic implications. Crises may arise which are not
> directly connected with the exploitation of petroleum but which
> are likely to affect these operations profoundly.
>
> The fact that actual and potential political difficulties exist
> does not mean that American corporations must or should abandon
> interests in this area which are in hand or which may be developed.
> It does mean, however, that constant contact with the political,
> economic and social developments needs to be maintained and that
> careful consideration be given to any changes in these factors which
> occur. . .

From the Intelligence Report:

> . . . Mr. Hayes, an irregation [sic] expert now in the employ of a
> Zionist organization in the U.S., has been working on a large scale
> irregation [sic] scheme for Palestine . . .
>
> Hayes' plan is to use all available water in the area—the Jordan,
> deep wells and surface reservoirs. He also contemplates using waters
> of the Letany [sic] river by diverting the flow through a tunnel into

Palestine. There is no reason to doubt the feasibility of Hayes' plan from a technical point of view as he has had previous experience in the field including the Tennessee Valley Authority Project . . .

It is felt that the possibility of such an irregation [sic] scheme will only be used as a further argument for Jewish immigration and any practical application of the plan is not considered for the present or anytime in the future.

For the historian, a full reading of these documents elicits a mine of multifaceted information. New interpretive dimensions are opened also by the interconnections between archival materials in American and Israeli repositories. The twin teams in the United States and Israel have continued to combine their findings, and their joint research has yielded important documentation on the innovative and far-reaching economic institutions of the Zionist Movement.

Relief aid was a dedicated practice of both the American government and organized Jewry, particularly during critical days for the Holy Land. Several important studies based on extant materials deal with the emergency assistance afforded to the virtually imprisoned Jewish population in Palestine during World War I, as it was caught in the crossfire and intrigues of the governing officials. Augmented sources from the archives of the Central Zionist Office in Berlin (later removed to the Central Zionist Archives in Jerusalem) include documentation on the effective American Jewish involvement during those awesome years. A highly informative report (typescript) by H. H. Cohn (February 1915) elaborates his thesis that "the educating power of the American (Relief) Fund lies in its organizing power" and highlights the efforts that flowed from such organization. Further significant material on the war-front relief activities is to be found in the records of the American Board of Commissioners for Foreign Missions, housed in the Houghton Library of Harvard University.

The Land of Israel, however, could not be rehabilitated only by relief, eleemosynary or philanthropic ventures. Jewish leaders in the United States had a special sense for economic enterprise and hoped to introduce American entrepreneurial and technological methods into Zionist dreams. Even Henrietta Szold, hardly an economic expert, dealt with proposals to carry out hybridization experiments on oranges that had been grown in California. The philosopher Horace Kallen engaged Felix Frankfurter, the jurist, in a plan to incorporate a company that was to have as its purpose the "establishment and development of agricultural and industrial enterprise in Palestine" (listed under Frankfurter, Felix).

Furthermore, these papers bear witness to the remarkable impact of Louis D. Brandeis on American Zionism and on the World Zionist Executive—an impact due in large measure to his economic acumen. As early as May 1912, Brandeis took formal leadership in creating the American Palestine Company, whose goal was to fortify the economy of the Holy Land. Nahum Sokolow, a preeminent member of the World Zionist Executive, wrote two years later (November 3, 1914) about the inaugural event in Boston. He recalled the "honor of introducing and assisting Mr. Brandeis' first and memorable appearance on a Zionist platform and the meetings arranged with Mr. Brandeis in New York with the great result of deciding the foundation of a great American Palestine Company." In an earlier letter (July 20, 1913) to Louis Lipsky, Chairman of the Executive Committee of the Federation of American Zionists, Sokolow proposed that Brandeis be invited to the "Präsidium" of the World Zionist Congress, thus endowing him with the "moral authority of the Congress. I should think that the Zionists of the United States have the right to be represented in the 'Präsidium' and that Mr. Brandeis will be the right man in the right place" (both listed under Central Zionist Office, Berlin).

Another impressive, but unfortunately all too little-known figure in Zionist history, was Emanuel Neumann. He devoted much of his ingenuity to practical economic enterprise, which he considered to be the cornerstone of political work. During the 1930s, Dr. Neumann, then Head of the Jewish Agency's Economic Department, was acutely concerned with facilitating the emigration of the threatened Jews of Germany to Palestine. He dealt forcefully with the issue of "absorptive capacity," which was raised as a primary reason for a paralyzing migration policy. In a letter to Senator William King in May 1933, Dr. Neumann argued, "It is not sufficient to permit a certain limited number of Jews to enter the country annually. . . . It is necessary to have some big plan behind which will be the Mandatory Government and the other Powers . . . "

Never an improvisor but always a far-reaching planner, Dr. Neumann worked earnestly to demonstrate the economic-absorptive potentialities of Palestine. One of his major projects was the "Economic Development Plan for Palestine—the Lowdermilk Project" (November 19, 1942), patterned after the Tennessee Valley Authority in the United States. Neumann approached Dr. W. C. Lowdermilk, then in Washington, to write a book on Palestine to be based largely on the studies Lowdermilk had undertaken on behalf of the U.S. Department of Agriculture in 1939. That book, *Palestine: Land of Promise*, contains a memorable chapter on the Jordan Valley Authority—a bold and ingenious vision. Emanuel Neumann maintained that it was "one of the most significant contributions ever made to Political Zionism."

These few selections from the economic and philanthropic citations in this volume illustrate the scope and method of our endeavor. We are assembling the scattered documents in order to assess and prepare them for scholarly inquiry and interpretation. Volume 4 is now being edited for publication by Menahem Kaufman and Mira Levine. Basically it is a supplementary volume to the previous books on American presence and diplomatic policy and Zionism. Its special significance, however, is the annotation of new record groups examined in British and Israeli repositories as well as the first findings in Turkish archives. Volume 5 will deal primarily with "Culture and Science" and "Christian Relations." We further expect that the results of the Second International Scholars Colloquium, to be held at the United States National Archives in the Fall of 1983, will yield another volume, including the papers and discussions of scholars from Great Britain, Israel, Turkey and the United States.

None of these projects could have been realized without the stalwart aid of such devotees of scholarship as Milton J. Krensky, of blessed memory, and his wife Rosemary Ehrenreich, friends of the Hebrew University's Institute of Contemporary Jewry from its very inception. Milton Krensky gave of his thought and substance to the program of America-Holy Land Studies. It is particularly appropriate that this volume on "Economic Relations and Philanthropy" be associated with Milton, for these subjects preoccupied his mind and heart as he worked valiantly to sustain Eretz Israel. He was convinced that the security of the world is based upon the sound economy of the world and that the future of the American and Israeli democracies depend upon it. He was particularly proud of establishing with Rosemary the Stephen S. Wise Chair in American Jewish Life and Institutions at the Institute. We gratefully dedicate this volume to the continuation of the life work of Milton J. Krensky.

Jerusalem, Israel   Moshe Davis
March, 1983

PART ONE
ECONOMIC RELATIONS

AGRON (AGRONSKY), GERSHON, 1893-1959

(Born in the Ukraine; moved to the United States in 1906; enlisted in Jewish Legion in 1918; resident of Palestine after demobilization except for 1921-1924; journalist and correspondent, founded and edited the *Palestine Post*; mayor of Jerusalem, 1955-1959.)
2 items, covering years 1920 and 1921, in Folder 12 in Record Group A209.
In Central Zionist Archives, Jerusalem.

The items are a letter to Agronsky dated January 26, 1921, from "The American-Palestine Mail Order House," regarding sale of Palestine products in the United States; and power of attorney signed by Abraham Goldberg of New York (June 1, 1920), "Secretary of the Palestine Carpet Company 'MARBADIAH,' " authorizing Agronsky to act in his stead in Palestine.
Material cataloged by repository.
Research access not restricted. Photocopies provided.

OZ 12/74

AMERICAN ECONOMIC COMMITTEE FOR PALESTINE

1.   2 boxes, covering years 1932-1948.
In Zionist Archives and Library, New York City.

Among the papers is found the following statement of purpose; "To be of practical assistance to Palestine industry and agriculture and to help create sound industrial, agricultural and commercial enterprises in Palestine to the end that employment opportunities may be created for new immigrants. The membership of the Committee comprises technical and business specialists and economists and professional men whose specialized experience can be used to help solve specific problems confronting Palestine's industry and agriculture. These specialists can also render specific assistance in the creation of new industries and in the development of markets for these industries in the Mid-East and elsewhere."

Includes minutes of the Executive Committee for May 10, 23, and June 13 (undated); pamphlets, including *Palestine Immigration: Dependents of Illegals, Palestine Arabs in the World War: Myth and Reality* and *The Refugee Problem and Palestine; Palestine Economic News* for 2/34 and 1/36; reports, including "Palestine as an Investment Field" (1933), "Progress for Industry in Palestine" (1934), "Diamond Industry" (1940), "Economic Aspects of Palestine" (undated) and "Brief Summary of Specific Activities of American Economic Committee for Palestine (AEC) (1944-1948); and various reports from other Jewish agencies concerning economic development (e.g., Jewish Agency, Municipality of Tel Aviv, etc.) Material not cataloged by repository.
Research access restricted. Permission needed to see Executive Committee minutes. Photocopies provided.

RM 6/73

2.   7 folders, covering years 1932-1948, in Robert Szold Papers (VI I-7).
In Zionist Archives and Library, New York City.

Includes minutes (in folders marked "Correspondence") of a general meeting to report on progress of the organization to 1/9/33, and of the work that needs to be done; of the Executive Committee (1932-1935, 1937) at which various projects were discussed; of the Administrative Committee (11/33, 9/37); and of the Board of Directors (1943-1945). Within these folders are also financial reports for 1932-1938.

Also contains material on fund raising; publication projects (*Agriculture Index, Industrial Index, PEN*); the establishment of the Mt. Vernon Palestine Corporation; a proposal for statistical investigations of industry, agriculture, and labor; agricultural and mining investments; a paper on Palestine Endowment Fund (December, 1932); a proposal to train, in the United States, boys and girls for farm work prior to *Aliyah*; the work of the Rockaways Palestine Corporation; the need to speed up colonization due to the situation developing in Germany (April, 1933); inquiries from Germany through the Hitachduth Olej Germania and from the Zionist Organization of Hungary for aid to immigration to Palestine (1933) with the AEC heading the Central Bureau of Palestine Organizations participating in this work; the British disregard for the Jewish claim to Palestine; a program for the development of the orange industry in Palestine; establishment of a bank to handle small-sized business loans; visit of American senators to Palestine; correspondence between the New (Revisionist) Zionist Organization and the Colonial Office and Royal Commission studying unfair treatment of Jews and the resumption of disturbances; a study of the banking situation in Palestine (1925-1937); demographic studies (1927); a paper, "Economic Consequences of Partition," and a Confidential Memo on the same subject (1937); establishing favorable customs tariffs with the United States; bringing Jewish capital out of Central and Eastern Europe; the question of Palestine's food supply in the face of a possible emergency situation (1940); war conditions in Palestine; and the establishment of the Economic Coordinating Committee for Palestine (July, 1945), of which the AEC, the Economic Bureau of the ZOA, and the American Office of the Jewish Agency were charter members, with minutes and summaries of reports and activities for June-October, 1945.

A folder marked "Press releases 1932-1933" contains position papers and speeches pertaining to economic developments in Palestine. Correspondents include Louis D. Brandeis, Israel Brodie, Maurice Bookstein, Robert Szold, Morris Rothenberg, Julian Mack and Rehavia Lewin-Epstein.
Material cataloged by repository.
Research access not restricted. Photocopies provided.

RM 1/75

AMERICAN PALESTINE COMPANY
1 item, dated 1921.
In Zionist Archives and Library, New York City.
Item consists of a stock certificate.
Material not cataloged by repository.
Research access not restricted. Photocopies provided.

RM 7/76

AMERICAN PALESTINE INSTITUTE, INC.
2 items, dated 1943, interspersed in Silver Archives (A Correspondence 4-2-2 and 4-2-3).
In The Temple, Cleveland, Ohio.
Contains a report, "The Economic Potentialities of Palestine," issued by the Institute and I. B. Berkson's "Proposal for Institute for Palestine Research and Reports."
Material not cataloged by repository.
Research access not restricted. Photocopies provided.

MF 1/75

AMERICAN PALESTINE TRADING CORPORATION
1 folder, covering years 1942-1947.
In Zionist Archives and Library, New York City.
Contains bulletins, financial reports, and pamphlets in which it is stated that the corporation was formed "to establish an American investment corporation . . . to issue and sell its own stock and bonds in United States dollars and to coordinate and centralize the handling of exports from the U.S.A. to Palestine, and, after the war, to act as the underwriters for Palestinian undertakings on the financial market in the United States."
Material not cataloged by repository.
Research access not restricted. Photocopies provided.

RM 6/73

ATKINS, PAUL, 1892-1977
(Financial counsel and consulting economist.)
22-page report, dated March, 1944, in Box 10, File 1 of collection.
In Historical Manuscripts, Sterling Memorial Library, Yale University, New Haven, Connecticut.
The 22-page "Report on Conditions in Syria, Lebanon, Palestine, Egypt, Transjordan, Iraq and Arabia," calls Palestine's economy unstable and precarious, predicts increasing hostilities between Jews and Arabs and suggests that businesses limit their commitments in the area until the situation improves.
Collection cataloged by repository.
Research access not restricted. Photocopies provided.

JDS 1/76

AUSTER, DANIEL, 1893-1963
(b. Stanislav, Galicia; arrived in Eretz Yisrael in 1914; appointed deputy mayor of Jerusalem by High Commissioner, 1935; acting mayor, 1936-1938, 1944-1945; elected mayor, 1948-1951.)
1 item, dated 1948, in Record Group A297.
In Central Zionist Archives, Jerusalem.

Folder 5 contains a letter dated February 3, 1948 from Dr. Fokchanner to Auster reporting that Jerusalem Diamond Ltd. (of which Auster was a director) had established commercial contacts with Mr. S. Morgenstein of New York. The Histadrut in Eretz Yisrael was a partner and Leon Wexler the New York agent of diamond exporters Jokl and Weinreich.
Collection cataloged by repository.
Research access not restricted. Photocopies provided.

SG 10/81

BANK LEUMI LE-ISRAEL
(Formerly Anglo-Palestine Company and Anglo-Palestine Bank, Jaffa and Tel Aviv; incorporated as Anglo-Palestine Company in London in 1902 as a subsidiary of the Jewish Colonial Trust to serve as a banking and financial instrument to further Zionist activity in Palestine.)
Ca. 150 items, covering years 1914-1917 and 1923-1924, interspersed in Record Group L51.
In Central Zionist Archives, Jerusalem.

The collection contains correspondence (May-August, 1914) between Louis Lipsky and Jacob De Haas to the Anglo-Palestine Bank concerning plans to organize the "American Palestine Company" (APC) led by Judge Brandeis to build up the Palestinian economy, especially in railway and port development (Folders 16 and 95). Of special interest is a letter from De Haas to Zalman David Levontin (June 5, 1914), outlining the principles upon which the company is to be based.

Folder 196 contains correspondence (1923-1924) by Siegfried Hoofien of APC with Bernard A. Rosenblatt about the latter's plan to float a loan in the United States for a group of Palestinian Jewish municipalities, which he advocated after the success of the Tel Aviv bond issue. Of special interest is a letter from Rosenblatt to Hoofien (October 5, 1923) in which he states that it is impossible to sell Palestine securities in the United States on a strictly business basis, but that some sentimental appeal must be part of the effort.

Folder 188 deals with the liquidation of an orange-packing plant in Petah-Tikva belonging to the "American Fruit Growers of Palestine, Inc.," 1923-1924.

Folders 86, 180, 181 and 182 contain correspondence and documents relating to a loan of approx. $40,000 (known as the "American Orange Loan"), provided between 1915 and 1917 by the ZOA to orange growers in Palestine who could not export their crops because of World War I. Folder 182 shows that the balance of the account was transferred to the Kupat-Milveh Society in Jerusalem via the Palestine Endowment Fund, Inc. Of special interest is a report (January 9, 1916) to the "Committee for the American Orange Loan," which contains a detailed history of the loan, its manner of implementation and the disbursement of funds to date.

Material cataloged by repository.

Research access not restricted. Photocopies provided.

YG 3/75

BERKSON, ISAAC B., 1891-1975
(American educator; member of Palestine Executive of the Jewish Agency, 1931-1935).
Ca. 30 items, covering years 1931-1936, 1941, in Record Group A348.
In Central Zionist Archives, Jerusalem.

The collection includes correspondence, receipts and financial reports on the following matters: management of the *Pardes* at Netanya owned jointly by the Berksons, Albert Schoolmans, Israel Chipkins and several other Americans, especially correspondence and financial statements from Hanoteah (Folders 9-12, 25, 28, 29, 68 and 100); and purchase of land in Bayit Vegan, Jerusalem, for the Hyman family in the United States (Folder 96, 97 and 100).

Of special interest is a 10-page report submitted by Emanuel Neumann, dated November 19, 1941, entitled "An Economic Development Plan for Palestine, Suggestions for a Survey and Report." Marked "Confidential," it stresses the importance of increasing the

absorption capacity of Eretz Yisrael for resolving the problem of settling refugees and realizing the goals of Zionism. Also mentioned are the Lowdermilk Project (Jordan Valley Authority patterned after the Tennessee Valley Authority in the United States); Vice-President Henry Wallace; a visit by Lowdermilk, David Lilienthal, Robert Szold, Israel Brodie and Neumann to the TVA project in Tennessee (Folder 18).
Collection cataloged by repository.
Research access not restricted. Photocopies provided.

ML 11/81

BEZALEL SCHOOL OF ARTS

(Founded in 1906 by Prof. Boris Schatz; trains students in arts and design, including painting, sculpture and home industries.)
Ca. 100 items, including two books, covering years 1906-1948, interspersed and in special folders (227/261; 216/122; 229/273; 222/146; 224/211) in M12.
In Jerusalem Municipality-Historical Archives, Jerusalem.

The collection contains letters and lists of contributors to the school, letters by Americans interested in studying at the school, and business correspondence by Americans who were interested in selling Bezalel art work in America.
Collection not cataloged by repository.
Research access not restricted. Photocopies provided.

RB 9/74

BRODIE, ISRAEL B., 1884-1965

(Born in Shavel, Lithuania; immigrated to Baltimore, Maryland in 1886; successful lawyer and businessman; cofounder of Palestine Economic Corporation and president of American Economic Committee.)
Ca. 5 linear feet, covering years 1930-1964, interspersed and in special folders in Record Group A251.
In Central Zionist Archives, Jerusalem.

Collection contains correspondence and reports of the American Economic Committee, the Palestine Potash Works, the Palestine Economic Committee and many other enterprises with which I. B. Brodie was involved.

Correspondence about the Palestine Potash Works is found in Folders 93-181. Of interest in Folder 106 are letters describing ways and means by which the Potash Company could help the U.S. war effort.

A large part of the collection relates to the American Economic Committee. A document describing its purposes is found in Folder 17/a. All other AEC correspondence and documents are in Folders 270-322, 324, 328 and 329/b. Of special interest is Folder 281, in which are found negotiations for trade agreements with the United States in 1938 to facilitate the export of citrus fruit to the United Kingdom; a letter in Folder 304 (January 13, 1935) from S. Sharnopolsky of the Palestine Health and Rest Resorts Comp. Ltd., describing the exhibit at the Chicago World's Fair (1934) and suggesting a Palestine House in New York to promote Palestine as a Health and Tourist Center; and Folder 329/b, which contains a copy of a letter to L. Brandeis from Brodie about the respected position of the AEC in Palestine; ". . . designated by the outstanding economic groups in Palestine as the official source of economic information."

The activities of the Palestine Economic Corporation are discussed in Folders 17/b and 185-269. Of special interest are the reports of the merger with the Palestine Co. (Folder 237/a); PEC interest in "Assis" (Folders 193 and 248); PEC interest in ATA Textile Co. Ltd. (Folders 187, 194 and 254); and PEC involvement with Bayside Housing (Folders 197 and 225). These latter folders contain correspondence dated July, 1947-February, 1948 about erecting a Freedom Village in the Bayside area, using all-aluminum prefabricated houses. Other folders in which low-cost and prefabricated housing is described are 240 and 303. Correspondence about the sale of Palestine products in the United States can be found in Folders 25, 36, 63/p, 247, 256, 301 and 315. Correspondence about developing a market for American products in Palestine is in Folder 256. Letters and reports about various economic enterprises, successful and unsuccessful, are noted in Folders 31, 63/b, 63/p, 64/g, 64/j, 64/l, 199, 215, 223, 234, 236, 247, 257, 288, 300, 301, 306, 308, 313, 315, 319, 328 and 329/a. Some of the ventures discussed are textiles, optics, false teeth, Coca-Cola, telephone, tobacco and tourism. References to the diamond industry are in

Folders 211 and 287. Correspondence involving the Palestine Water Co. is found in Folders 261/a, 261/b and 261/c. Problems of shipping and ports in Palestine are discussed in Folders 29 and 216. Letters and reports concerning oil and the Middle East are in Folders 21 and 325. Of interest in Folder 325 is a letter to Brandeis from F. Julius Fohs (June 4, 1924) re Fohs's tentative plan for Palestine land and exploration companies.

Correspondence with Edward A. Norman (Folder 17/a) contains information about natural gas in Palestine, Palestine hotels, improved fruit wrappers (also discussed in Folder 310) and the Palestine Investment Co. This subject is also found in Folder 22. The possibilities of growing sugar cane or sugar beets in Palestine are discussed in correspondence in Folder 28.

The correspondence file of Felix Frankfurter (Folder 63/c) contains several economic reports. Economic reports by Brodie are also found in Folders 63/0, 317 and 327. Reports and correspondence about banks and banking in Palestine are found in Folders 33, 63/p, 188, 244, and 299. The collection also contains correspondence from Stephen S. Wise about economic problems and Jewish Agency participation in the AEC budget. Of interest in this folder is a letter from Brodie to Wise (May 24, 1938), explaining why Brodie does not contribute to the United Palestine Appeal (Folder 320). Tourist traffic to Palestine is the subject of Folder 321. The possibility of developing a magnesium metal industry near the Dead Sea is discussed in Folder 16, and a pamphlet called "The Dead Sea Concession" is found in Folder 50.
Material cataloged by repository.
Research access not restricted. Photocopies provided.

OZ 1/75

2.   1 box, covering years 1929-1941.
In Zionist Archives and Library, New York City.
Contains correspondence concerning the open-door policy for immigration and other British policies toward Palestine, labor conditions in Palestine, Arab reactions to the presence of Jewish immigrants including the riots and boycott, American economic interests in Palestine (e.g., Palestine Economic Corporation), economic and industrial development in Palestine and ZOA internal

affairs.   Correspondents include Dr. Bernhardt, Louis D. Brandeis, Pinhas Rutenberg, Julian Mack, E. N. Mohl, Robert Szold and Jacob De Haas.
Material not cataloged by repository.
Research access not restricted. Photocopies provided.

RM 2/75

CENTRAL ZIONIST OFFICE, BERLIN
(Moved from Cologne to Berlin in 1911 because most members of the Inner Actions Committee elected at the 10th Zionist Congress resided there; absorbed the Commission for the Exploration of Palestine and the Palestine Department, which had led a separate existence in Berlin since 1903; transferred to London after the annual conference of 1920.)
Ca. 10 items, covering years 1913-1916, interspersed in Record Group Z3.
In Central Zionist Archives, Jerusalem.
The relevant correspondence deals with the proposed American Palestine Company initiated by Brandeis (Folders 755, 757 and 761). Of special interest is a letter dated May 21, 1914 from Louis Lipsky to David Levontin, manager of the Anglo-Palestine Bank, requesting information about the feasibility of an intercolony railroad, docks and dock terminals, other transportation facilities, waterworks and special industries as possible investments for the company organized by Brandeis "for taking up in Palestine some enterprise that shall have national value and significance to the Jewish people" (Folder 757).
A few letters in Folders 385 and 761 deal with the possible sale of Palestinian products in the United States.
Collection cataloged by repository.   (Record Group description available as mimeographed volume).
Research access not restricted. Photocopies provided.

OZ 6/75

FRANKEL, LEE KAUFER, 1867-1931
(Prominent American social worker and insurance executive.)
Ca. 500 items, covering years 1918-1931, interspersed in collection (P-146).

In American Jewish Historical Society, Waltham, Massachusetts.
Contains 22 items relating to the Palestine Economic Corporation (president, Bernard Flexner; vice-presidents, Herbert Lehman and Louis Marshall; secretary, Joseph Hyman). Includes a list of members to December 15, 1939; a statement of plan and purpose ("the Palestine Economic Corporation has been formed to afford an instrument through which American Jews and others who are desirous of cooperating may be helpful in supplying capital and credit on a business basis to productive Palestinian commercial, industrial, agricultural and other kindred enterprises and thereby further the economic development of the Holy Land and the settlement there of an increasing number of Jews"); correspondence regarding investors (especially with Julius Rosenwald and Lord Melchett); the 1928 annual report describing the following activities: the Haifa Bay Land Purchase, agriculture credits, orange marketing, industrial credits, housing projects and a hotel (total investment—$2,300,000); and the treasurer's report of January 14, 1929.

Also contains five documents relating to the 1929 Jewish Agency Financial Corporation (Felix Warburg, ex officio; Lee K. Frankel, chairman; Committee: Julian Mack, Israel B. Brodie, Edmund I. Kaufman, Aaron Strauss and Bernard Flexner) including a draft memorandum, suggested activities, the minutes of the meeting of September 26, 1929, lists of participants and nonparticipants and a letter (March 12, 1930) describing the decision to merge into an expanded Palestine Economic Corporation.

The most important part of the collection is contained in 9 files (Box 22) on the Non-Partisan Survey of Palestine (1927-1928) designed "to make a scientific and thorough Survey and Investigation of the Agricultural, Industrial, Commercial, Economic and Financial condition of Palestine and adjacent countries and related subjects." Joining Frankel on the commission were Sir Alfred Mond (London), Felix Warburg and Oscar Wasserman (Berlin). In addition to correspondence with witnesses and commission aides, notably Dr. Milton J. Rosenau, Louis Marshall, Frederick H. Kisch and Bernard Flexner, the papers include staff reports, records, newspaper clippings and the final commission report, which stresses methods for making the country economically viable through the use of sound business practices. A £1 million budget was proposed.

In addition, the collection contains some letters on Zionism and non-Zionism; correspondence regarding the Non-Partisan Conference to consider Palestine Problems (1925–Louis Marshall, chairman) and the 1927 Weizmann-Marshall dinner; a list of non-Zionists appointed to the Council of the Jewish Agency (June 12, 1931) and the text of Frankel's address to the Jewish Agency in 1931 (Box 2).

Material cataloged by repository.

Research access not restricted. Photocopies provided.

JDS 6/75

FRIEDENWALD, HARRY, 1864-1950

(Medical doctor, longtime active Zionist; president and honorary president of the Federation of American Zionists, 1904-1918; acting chairman of the Zionist Commission in Palestine, 1919; visited Palestine on various occasions.)

42 items, covering years 1911-1942, interspersed in folders in Record Group A182.

In Central Zionist Archives, Jerusalem.

Folders 4, 8/6 and 53 contain correspondence relating to Friedenwald's numerous investments in Palestine, primarily his orchards. Of special interest is a map of Friedenwald's property in Birkat Eitan (Folder 53).

Material cataloged by repository.

Research access not restricted. Photocopies provided.

TzB 2/75

GENERAL MORTGAGE BANK OF PALESTINE

1 box, covering years 1925-1938.

In Zionist Archives and Library, New York City.

Contains correspondence between the Committee on the General Mortgage Bank (appointed by the Administrative Committee of the ZOA) and the Palestine Zionist Executive to investigate the bank and establish terms upon which they would recommend ZOA, Keren Hayesod and the American Zion Commonwealth investment in it; copies of the bank's prospectus and bonds and annual accounts for 1926-1934 and 1938.

Material not cataloged by repository.
Research access not restricted. Photocopies provided.

RM 2/75

GREAT BRITAIN, FOREIGN OFFICE. GENERAL CORRESPON-
DENCE AFTER 1906; POLITICAL CORRESPONDENCE OF THE
POLITICAL DEPARTMENT
320 items, covering years 1939-1945, interspersed in collection
(F0371).
In Public Record Office, London, England.

Although the major relevance of this collection is in the area
of political relations, economic matters of actual or potential
political value are scrutinized. Subjects brought to the attention
of the Foreign Office by the British ambassador in Washington, the
British consul-general in New York, the British high commissioner
in Palestine and the American ambassador to London are discussed,
the documents being correspondence from officials or companies,
informational or historical background material and interdepart-
mental minutes speculating on political repercussions. The two main
topics dealt with concern American trade relations with Palestine
and the American Palestine Institute.

Discussion with the Italian representative, Signor Crolla, about
Italian trading rights with Palestine drew attention to the special
status enjoyed by the United States. As a member of the League of
Nations, Italy was entitled to most-favored-nation rights. The
question raised by the Italian Government pertained to the attitude
of His Majesty's Government (HMG) toward according Italy trading
rights upon termination of her membership in the League on
December 11, 1939. The resulting investigation of this inquiry
centered upon the United States as a precedent or an exception
(FO 371/23251).

On November 16, 1939 the Marquess of Lothian, then British
ambassador to the United States, reported that the U.S. State
Department was not treating Palestine as a belligerent in the war;
consequently there would be no restrictions on American vessels
trading in Palestine ports (FO 371/23251). Another topic of concern
dealt with the potentially explosive issue of the Palestine Import
and License Control that the Palestine Government intended to

impose. The U.S. State Department took great exception to any legislation in trade matters that might reduce imports from the United States, seeing such restrictions as a violation of Article 2 of the American-British Mandate Convention of December 3, 1924 and of Article 18 of the mandate, which assured American trade with Palestine equality of treatment with that of the Mandatory Power or of any foreign state. Subsequent consultation within the British policy-making bodies encompassed the Colonial Office, the High Commissioner, the British Board of Trade, the British Ambassador to the United States, the Treasury, and the U.S. Ambassador to the United Kingdom (FO 371/24566).

A letter of January 17, 1944 from W. G. Hayter of the British Embassy in Washington supplied the Eastern Department of the Foreign Office with background information about the American Palestine Institute. The Institute was described as an independent body consisting of Zionist-inclined Jewish economists and government officials, including Benjamin Cohen, Isador Lubin and Louis Bean. The aim of the Institute was to investigate the economic potentialities of Palestine to ascertain if the country is "capable of supporting a substantially larger population than its present one, at a standard of living which could attract such a population—having regard to the probable pressures upon Jews to seek new homes." Much of the documentation is concerned with the Institute's planned visit to Palestine (FO 371/40142 and /45408).

The collection also contains information on the Palestine Economic Corporation, whose capital reserves and surpluses were in reported excess of $3,500,000, its American stockholders numbering 1,400 and its aim since its foundation in 1926 to enable American Jewish investment in Palestine to further its economic development and resettlement of Jews (FO 371/45408).

Collection indexed by repository.

Research access not restricted. Photocopies provided.

EE 5/75

GROSSMAN, MEIR, 1888-1964
(Born in Russia; journalist and Zionist Revisionist leader; founded *Jerusalem Bulletin* (later *Palestine* then *Jerusalem Post*.)
4 items, covering years 1933, 1936-1937, in Record Group P59.

In Jabotinsky Institute in Israel, Tel Aviv.

The items consist of correspondence regarding a request from Grossman for a list of the American shareholders of the Jewish Colonial Trust (Folder 2/62); the decision by Harry Mottsmann of the Distillers Products Corporation of America to undertake the distribution of wines from Eretz Yisrael in the United States; and the effect of Prohibition in America on the wine industry in Eretz Yisrael (Folder 2/100/5).

Collection cataloged by repository.

Research access not restricted. Photocopies available.

TG 12/81

GRUENWALD, KURT, 1901-1975
(Banker, economist, public figure in Jerusalem.)
Ca. 15 items, covering years 1934, 1937, and 1939, in Record Group A343.
In Central Zionist Archives, Jerusalem.

The collection includes memoranda and correspondence regarding American Jewish interest in the commercial and industrial development of Eretz Yisrael. There is an account of meetings in April-May, 1934 with Justice Felix Frankfurter attended by Julius Simon, Rehavia Lewin-Epstein, Muhamed Yunis Husseini and the treasurer of the Mandatory Government. At the May 28, 1934 meeting, Frankfurter spoke highly of the American Economic Bureau for Palestine and of Rehavia Lewin-Epstein. Gruenwald praised Lewin-Epstein and Simon as the first Americans to gain "the goodwill and esteem of all factions of the Yishuv and of gentiles as well" (Folder 2).

Problems of industrial credit in Eretz Yisrael and attempts by Edward Norman to mobilize American capital for the Palestine Economic Corporation are discussed in Folder 4.

A 168-page mimeographed report by Gruenwald, entitled "Army Supplies Industry in Palestine" (1939), lists manufacturers and dealers of army supplies and sources of raw materials, including numerous imports from the United States (Folder 1).

Collection cataloged by repository.

Research access not restricted. Photocopies provided.

ML 2/81

HAKIBBUTZ HAMEUHAD. SECRETARIAT
2 items, dated 1946, in Record Group 1A.
In Hakibbutz Hameuhad Archives, Ramat Ef'al, Ramat Gan.

The items are two letters in Hebrew from the secretariat of the American consul general concerning a business trip to the United States by Aharon Meged: request for a business/visitor visa for Meged to purchase and send equipment to Hakibbutz Hameuhad Publishers and to negotiate the publication and translation of several of their books; certification that Hakibbutz Hameuhad Publishers will cover the full cost of passage and maintenance in the United States for Meged (Folder 102).
Collection cataloged by repository.
Research access not restricted. Photocopies provided.

TG 6/81

HISTORY OF THE YISHUV
4 items and scattered references in press bulletins, covering the 1920s and 1938-1943, in Record Group 4.
In Yad Ben Zvi Archives, Jerusalem.

The items consist of statistical information on trade between the United States and Eretz Yisrael interspersed in monthly bulletins published by the Office of Statistics, 1938 and 1943 (Folder 4/3/12,21); a printed report of the Trade and Industry Department of the Jewish Agency in the 1920s, recorded in bulletins published by the Zionist Press Commission, *Yediot Me-Eretz Yisrael* (in Hebrew) and *Palestine Correspondence*, containing lists of newly certified Jewish companies (Folder 4/3/15-16).
Computerized index to 4/2/1-5 only.   Remainder of collection classified but not cataloged.
Research access not restricted. Photocopies provided.

AF 2/82

JABOTINSKY, ERI, 1910-1969
(Son of Zev Jabotinsky; active associate of Peter Bergson in the United States during World War II.)
4 items, dated 1948, in Record Group A4.
In Jabotinsky Institute in Israel, Tel Aviv.

The items consist of correspondence with Earle Spessard regarding a serious attempt in Jerusalem to produce hydroponic vegetables.
Collection not cataloged by repository.
Research access not restricted. Photocopies provided.

SA 1/82

JABOTINSKY, ZEV (VLADIMIR), 1880-1940
(Internationally prominent Zionist; soldier, author and poet; founder of the Zionist Revisionist Movement; played a leading role in the establishment of the Jewish Legion in World War I and served as a lieutenant in the unit.)
7 items, covering years 1922-1934, in Record Group A 1.
In Jabotinsky Institute in Israel, Tel Aviv.

The collection contains reports by Jabotinsky as Palestine director of the New York-based Judea Insurance Company to its board of directors on problems and developments in the Palestine office and various suggestions for improvement (Volume 34, pp. 257, 260 and 315).

Of special interest is a letter (February 11, 1934) from Jabotinsky to Eliahu Ginsburg of the Metropolitan Life Insurance Company, proposing a plan to increase the number of *Aliyah* certificates granted to potential Revisionist settlers, who often lacked the necessary one-year assurance of employment because they were not members of the Histadrut. Jabotinsky requested that the insurance company try to convince the Mandatory Government to accept the company's two-year unemployment insurance policy for *halutzim* who did not have definite employment (Volume 37, p. 899). Also included is correspondence between Jabotinsky and the Palestine Development Council and Pinhas Rutenberg regarding power plants for Eretz Yisrael (Volume 4).
Collection cataloged by repository.
Research access not restricted. Photocopies provided.

ML/SA 4/82

JEWISH AGENCY, AGRICULTURAL SETTLEMENT DEPART-MENT, JERUSALEM
(The department responsible for initiating and aiding Jewish agricultural settlement in Eretz Yisrael.)

4 items, dated 1933, interspersed in Record Group S15.
In Central Zionist Archives, Jerusalem.

The items, all in Folder 3163, are reports and correspondence concerning the American Economic Committee for Palestine. Of interest is a 13-page report (August 10, 1933) on the organization and activities of the Committee.

Collection cataloged by repository.

Research access not restricted. Photocopies provided.

OZ 12/75

JEWISH AGENCY, ECONOMIC DEPARTMENT, JERUSALEM, 1931-1933

(The department, organized to coordinate investments and economic undertakings in Jewish Palestine, was headed by Emanuel Neumann during its short existence.)

Ca. 2 inches, covering years 1931-1933, interspersed and in special folders in Record Group S17.

In Central Zionist Archives, Jerusalem.

The bulk of the relevant material in the collection is correspondence and documents dealing with the activities of the American Economic Committee for Palestine and includes reports about Palestinian industry, possible exports to the United States and queries and suggestions about American investments in Palestine (Folders 74, 101, 102, 103, 126, 161 and 162). Folders 16 and 111 contain correspondence with M. Lieberman, an American sanitary engineer, who was interested in investing in public utilities in Tel Aviv, specifically the installation and operation of a sewage system. Folder 144 contains a letter from David L. Goldberg of Hartford, Connecticut, inquiring into the feasibility of establishing a small commercial radio station in Jerusalem, and a reply by Emanuel Neumann. Other queries about investments by Americans are in Folders 99, 144 and 163.

Folder 138 contains correspondence with the American consul and vice-consul in Jerusalem, 1932-1933, about the economic situation in Palestine and Folder 3 contains a copy of a letter (May 17, 1933) from Emanuel Neumann to Senator William King about the relative prosperity of Palestine despite the world depression.

Collection cataloged by repository.
Research access not restricted. Photocopies provided.

OZ 10/75

JEWISH AGENCY, GENERAL SECRETARIAT, 1920-1939
Ca. 45 items, covering years 1932-1937, interspersed and in special
folders in Record Group S30.
In Central Zionist Archives, Jerusalem.

All the material in this collection is concerned with the opening
of the office of the American Economic Committee for Palestine
in Tel-Aviv (Folders 2409/א; 2409/א; 2427; 805).
Material cataloged by repository.
Research access not restricted. Photocopies provided.

OZ 11/75

JEWISH AGENCY, POLITICAL DEPARTMENT, JERUSALEM,
1921-1948
(The department of the Jewish Agency—until 1929, the Palestine
Zionist Executive—which dealt directly with the government of
Palestine.)
Ca. 250 items, covering the years 1924-1947, interspersed and in
special folders in Record Group S25.
In Central Zionist Archives, Jerusalem.

The collection contains documents and correspondence concerning the economic activities of American companies in Palestine,
the sale of Palestinian products in the United States and visits to
Palestine by American businessmen and economic and labor experts.
Correspondence with and about the American-Palestine Line, Inc.
(shipping) and American Express Co. (telegraphic services) is found
in Folder 502; that concerning various other commercial companies
interested in trade with Jewish Palestine in Folder 7389. The
proposed visit (1924) of H. M. Smith, representing Standard Oil of
New York, the Du Pont Power Co. of Wilmington, Delaware and
General Motors, to take back samples of Dead Sea water for analysis
is documented in Folder 357.

Many folders include material about the activities of companies
established in the United States to further the economic development
of the *Yishuv*: the Palestine Economic Corporation (Folders 684,

1133 and 1151); correspondence of the American Economic Committee for Palestine, 1936-1938, including attempts to get the U.S. government to intervene with Great Britain for preferential treatment of Palestine products (Folders 5701 and 5731); the founding of the America-Palestine Trading Company—AMPAL (1944) and its early years (Folder 7389).

Material on the proposed Palestine commercial exhibits at the New York World's Fair (1939) is found in Folder 7351. Delegations of American businessmen to Palestine are described in Folders 512 (1927—led by Max Shoolman) and 7389 (1946—Fred Monosson). The views of Dr. Leo Wolman on the labor and economic situation in Palestine, 1927, are noted in Folder 8019. Problems concerning the repayment (1928) of a bond issue floated in the United States a few years earlier for the Tel Aviv Municipality are documented in Folder 9952.

Collection cataloged by repository.

Research access not restricted. Photocopies provided.

OZ 5/76

JEWISH AGENCY, TECHNICAL DEPARTMENT
Ca. ½ inch, covering years 1945-1949, interspersed and in special folders in Record Group S14.
In Central Zionist Archives, Jerusalem.

The bulk of this collection contains primarily correspondence (January 22, 1946-January 3, 1949) between the Palestine Purchasing Service and the Jewish Agency about purchasing building materials such as iron sheets, pipes, timber and plywood (Folder 99). Folder 168 also contains correspondence, blueprints and photographs about prefabricated houses and the possibilities of importing them to Eretz Yisrael.

Collection cataloged by repository.

Research access not restricted. Photocopies provided.

OZ 11/75

JEWISH NATIONAL FUND OF AMERICA
1 box, covering years 1921-1948.
In YIVO Institute for Jewish Research, New York City.

Contains the minutes of the Committee on Publicity and Propaganda of August, 1921, established to monitor the American-Arab press, fund-raising materials, a circular of activities for 1948, clippings and miscellaneous correspondence. The published materials include the *Shekel Bulletin* of the Labor Zionist and Progressive Bloc attending the 22nd World Zionist Congress (April 12, 1946-May 3, 1946); *Subduing the Emek*, by Elias Epstein (1923); *35 Years of Keren Kayemeth* (1937); *Our Struggle on Palestine's Seacoast and the Land Front* (1946); and *Crisis and Achievement—7 Years Struggle Against the Palestine Land Edict* (1946).
Material not cataloged by repository.
Research access not restricted. Photocopies provided.

RM 2/73

JEWISH PALESTINE PAVILION OF THE NEW YORK WORLD'S FAIR, 1939.
2 boxes, covering years 1939-1945.
In Zionist Archives and Library, New York City.
Contains promotional material describing the exhibits, financial papers and correspondence (including that of Meyer Weisgal).
Material not cataloged by repository.
Research access not restricted. Photocopies provided.

RM 6/73

JOSEPH, DOV (BERNARD), 1899-1981
(Born in Canada; settled in Jerusalem in 1921 after serving in the Jewish Legion during World War I; legal adviser, then member of Jewish Agency Executive.)
1 item, dated 1923, in Record Group 5/4.
In Yad Yitzhak Ben Zvi, Jerusalem.
The item is an issue (September 1, 1923) of the *Palestine Progress*, the monthly bulletin of the Palestine Development League, which contains information on economic developments in Eretz Yisrael and activities of Palestine Development Leagues in various cities in the United States (Folder 5/4/2/27).
Collection cataloged by repository.
Research access not restricted. Photocopies provided.

AF 4/82

JUDEA INDUSTRIAL CORPORATION
1 folder, dated 1926.
In YIVO Institute for Jewish Research, New York City.
    Contains miscellaneous correspondence for 1926.
Material not cataloged by repository.
Research access not restricted. Photocopies provided.

RM 2/73

KALLEN, HORACE M., 1882-1974
(Internationally prominent American-Jewish philosopher and edu-
cator.)
5 folders, covering years 1922-1948.
In YIVO Institute for Jewish Research, New York City.
    The collection contains material relating to the American
Economic Committee for Palestine (including news releases entitled
"Current Rapid Palestine Development Described"), the Palestine
Development Council (including letters to Jacob De Haas [1922]
concerning financial conditions in Palestine), the Palestine Develop-
ment League and the Palestine Economic Corporation.
Bibliographic description published by repository.
Research access not restricted. Photocopies provided.

RM 11/75

KESSELMAN, ROBERT DAVID, 1881-1942
(Born in Russia, arrived in the United States in 1901; certified public
accountant and comptroller of Zionist Organization of America;
emigrated to Palestine in 1919; first employed by Department of
Public Works, and after 1926 established accounting firm.)
17 items, covering years 1922 and 1936, interspersed in Record
Group A168.
In Central Zionist Archives, Jerusalem.
    Folder 9 contains correspondence between Kesselman and Dr.
Harry Friedenwald concerning Kesselman's handling of Friedenwald's
Palestine investments. Folder 13 (Kesselman's biography) includes
a description of a plan proposed by American Zionists to purchase
large tracts of land near Beer-Sheba. Folder 3 contains a letter to
Frank Katz about real estate investment opportunities, possibilities

for opening a hat shop and some material about the American Zion Commonwealth.
Material cataloged by repository.
Research access not restricted. Photocopies provided.

TzB 1/75

LEWIN-EPSTEIN, ELIAHU ZEEV, 1863-1932
(Arrived in the United States in 1900 and established Carmel Wine Company, went to Palestine in 1918 as member of Jewish Legion, returned to the United States on behalf of Bezalel, settled in Palestine in 1932.)
Ca. 40 items, covering years 1901-1929, interspersed and in special folders in Record Group A216.
In Central Zionist Archives, Jerusalem.

Folder 36 contains letters dealing with the establishment of Carmel Wine Co. in the United States between 1901 and 1916. Of interest is a notarized letter from Rishon le Zion Wine Cellars to the public of New York and other cities in the United States (February 22, 1901) announcing that Carmel Wines are now available in the United States. Also of interest in this folder is a letter dated August 21, 1916 from the Department of State to the American Chargé d'Affaires in London, introducing Lewin-Epstein, treasurer of the Provisional Executive Committee for General Zionist Affairs, who was going to London to make arrangements for exportation of products of the Jewish Colonies in Palestine.

Folder 6 contains letters concerning sale of wine in the United States (1915-1916). The collection also contains letters and documents dated January 6, 1920 to October 24, 1929 about the Jerusalem Art Store and "Amanuth," which sold Bezalel art products in America (Folder 22).
Material cataloged by repository.
Research access not restricted. Photocopies provided.

OZ 12/74

LEWIN-EPSTEIN, REHAVIA
(Son of Eliahu Zeev Lewin-Epstein; national secretary of Jewish Legion for Palestine in the United States in 1915; in Palestine in 1932 as employee of American Economic Committee for Palestine.)

Ca. 10 items, covering years 1932-1933, in special folder in Eliahu Zeev Lewin-Epstein Collection (Record Group A216).
In Central Zionist Archives, Jerusalem.

Folder 63 contains correspondence between Rehavia Lewin-Epstein and the American Economic Committee for Palestine concerning business and industrial development in Palestine.
Material cataloged by repository.
Research access not restricted. Photocopies provided.

OZ 12/74

LIEBERMAN, DAVID
1 box, covering years 1904-1911.
In Zionist Archives and Library, New York City.

Contains material dealing with the Maccabean Publishing Company, including minutes of the Annual Meeting of the Stockholders and of the Board of Directors, Stockholders Report (1910), financial reports, contracts, checks, advertising receipts, income tax form (1911) and the legal papers leasing the *Maccabaean* to Louis Lipsky and Bernard G. Richards. Includes also correspondence from Henrietta Szold, G. H. Mayer, Louis Lipsky, Jacob De Haas and the Zionist Council of Greater New York; a souvenir of the Kadimah Banquet held in New York City in 1904; and an interesting letter (1908) from a "Gentile," which reads as follows:

Gentlemen:

Inclose a P.O.O. for two dollars: One dollar for renewal of the "Maccabaean" for coming year and one dollar for the cause of Zionism as you may decide.

I appreciate the "Maccabaean" very much and all the more because of the increased Spirituality of its tone. Although a "Gentile" I am not as the Gentiles with which you may be familiar. My hope is in the Covenants which God made with Abraham and David. The gentiles hate what I believe as much as they hate the Jew. The Bible promises nothing to the Gentile as such. From time to time I see by the "Maccabaean" that you understand many prophecies just as I do. I often wonder if you recognize your whereabouts, that is as to time, in the Divine Programme. I rarely see a Jew and they cannot read English. All I have met are Zionists—and much they wonder to find one in me. Do not be too much disheartened. The time of your restoration to your own land Zion is not so very far in the future. The Near East will soon undergo a great change. Be ready for it. In the full assurance of the glorious fulfillment of your Prophecies and your own most glorious destiny, I am yours truly, James Laird

Material not cataloged by repository.
Research access not restricted. Photocopies provided.

RM 1/75

MACK, JULIAN WILLIAM, 1866-1943
(U.S. judge; prominent Jewish communal figure and Zionist leader; a founder of American Jewish Committee; president of American Jewish Congress, 1918; president of Zionist Organization of America, 1918; Israeli settlement Ramat ha-Shofet named in his memory.)
1 linear foot, covering years 1910-1947.
In Zionist Archives and Library, New York City.

The collection contains the following material relating to economic relations between America and the Holy Land: a folder labeled "Palestine Department: Investment Corporations" containing materials to assist in the creation of such local corporations and including a capital stock certificate of the Palestine Investment Company; circular letters of the ZOA containing "Plans for the Development of Local Palestine Investment Corporations," a sample Contract of Subscription and Agreement with Promoter, and a report of the Palestine Department regarding these corporations; a report of the ZOA Palestine Clearing Bureau (November, 1920-March, 1921); the By-Laws of the Palestine-Zion Investment Corporation, Zionist District #1, New York City; the Constitution and By-Laws, and a brief description of the American Palestine Engineering Construction Corporation; the By-Laws of the Palestine Investment Corporation of the Bronx; an outline of the By-Laws for Proposed Palestine Investment Corporation of Philadelphia; and a draft of the By-Laws for the Hudson Zion Colony.

Included among the Jewish Colonial Trust material (which contains the Articles of Association of the Trust and correspondence concerning American investments in its operation) is the certificate of incorporation of the American-Palestine Homestead and Development Company, Inc., whose stated purpose was to "take, buy, purchase, exchange, hire, lease or otherwise acquire real estate and property either improved or unimproved, and any interest or right therein, and to own, hold, control, maintain, manage and develop the same, in any State of the United States, and in any foreign country, particularly Palestine."

Correspondence and Memoranda for the Palestine Development Council (1923-1925) is concerned with Mack's findings in Palestine during his Middle East trip and Jacob De Haas's correspondence and excerpted diary of his Palestine trip (September, 1924-February, 1925); also included are the report of the meeting of the Board of the Central Bank of Cooperative Institutions in Palestine (July 2, 1923) and a copy of its Second Annual Report (year ending August 31, 1924); the Palestine Electric Corporation prospectus, detailed reports on the Rutenberg project, and correspondence from Rutenberg and others concerning the PDC's support of the project; and a verbatim transcription of the several sessions and addresses of the council's Second Annual Conference (May 27, 1923).

Correspondence and Memoranda of the Kupat Milveh (The Loan Bank, Ltd.) concerns its takeover by the newly formed Palestine Cooperative Company, the latter's formation with the inclusion of JDC assets in Kupat Milveh and of the JDC representatives on the PDC board of directors, and the financial activities for the years 1924-1927, among them the development of land on Mount Scopus (including a confidential report on the difficulties involved in dealing with unscrupulous persons in purchasing land in Palestine) and the Jewish Agricultural Experiment Station, which involved the Palestine Building Loan and Saving Association, Ltd. Also included are the financial statements for October 1, 1925-March 21, 1927.

The Palestine Economic Corporation files contain correspondence relating to its activities and that of the PCC, including the agreement to merge the two in 1926; a copy of "Palestine Electric Corporation, Ltd: Memorandum and Articles of Association, 1921"; a brochure entitled "Statement of The Plan and Purpose of the Palestine Economic Corporation"; the Annual Report of 1944; a copy of a memorandum of their activities submitted by the PEC to the United Nations Special Committee on Palestine (June 19, 1947);

and a letter by Robert Szold concerning the persons and events surrounding the history of the PEC.

The Palestine Cooperative Company material contains correspondence, including that of the Palestine Endowment Fund, concerning financial activities (including the Rutenberg Project); materials dealing with the sale of stocks and bonds; financial statements for 1923-1926; and minutes of the Board of Directors meeting for July 3, 1924, of a general meeting held in Chicago on January 5, 1924 and of an Administrative Committee for November 20, 1923.

Material cataloged by repository.

Research access not restricted. Photocopies provided.

RM 1/75

MANDATORY GOVERNMENT, CHIEF SECRETARY'S OFFICE (1918-1925)

3 items, covering years 1920 and 1922, in Folders M3 and 145 in Record Group 2.

In Israel State Archives, Jerusalem

The items concern a proposal by American Zionists submitted to Julius Simon by Bernard Flexner for the establishment of a land bank for rural and urban credit with its seat in Eretz Yisrael; a banquet of the American Palestine Company on December 19, 1921 attended by many important businessmen who signed a resolution to support the industrial rehabilitation of Eretz Yisrael (Bulletin number 38); and a report, "Trade and Industry in Palestine" (1922), stating that the American Palestine Iron Works Factory manufactured various types of machinery and employed 40 Arab and Jewish workers (Bulletin number 109).

Collection cataloged by repository. Published catalog available.

Research access not restricted. Photocopies provided.

TG 4/81

MANDATORY GOVERNMENT, DEPARTMENT OF AGRICULTURE AND FISHERIES

5 items, covering years 1936 and 1947, in Record Group 7.

In Israel State Archives, Jerusalem.

The collection contains a report for the 1936 Levant Fair in Tel Aviv, indicating the number and classification of American exhibits (Folder 42), and correspondence regarding the rejection by British authorities of a request by WIZO officials from Tel Aviv in 1947 to study agriculture and gardening in the United States (Folder 73).

Collection cataloged by repository.

Research access not restricted. Photocopies provided.

DF 3/82

MANDATORY GOVERNMENT, DEPARTMENT OF COMMERCE AND INDUSTRY

Ca. 3 linear feet, covering years 1942-1948, in Record Group 9.
In Israel State Archives, Jerusalem.

The collection includes letters, accounts and lists concerning British restrictions on the importation of goods and machinery to Eretz Yisrael from the United States and efforts by the Jewish Agency to lessen the impact of these restrictions (Folders DC 1/4-0-6/3; DC 1/4-0-6/4; DC 1/4-0-16/0), details of import licenses for American goods granted (Folders DC 1/4-0-16/0A, 0B, 0C; DC 1/4-0-16/1-25, 51-300, 316-356), and requests to the Mandatory authorities by Jewish and Arab individuals and companies to import goods and equipment from the United States (Folders DC I/1-6-11/11; DC I/3-1-7; DC I/4-0-6; DC I/4-0-6/5; DC I/4-21-18; DC I/4-24-0/2; DC I/4-42-0/1; DC I/4-42-0/3; DC I/4-50-0/1; DC I/6-12-0/1).

An explanation of British economic policy by the acting commissioner of the Department of Commerce and Industry to the Jewish Chamber of Commerce and his request to businessmen in Eretz Yisrael to import and export within the Sterling Bloc and not with other countries, such as the United States, are found in Folder DC I/1-6-4/15; British policy for granting licenses to import American goods is in Folders DC I/4-0-6A; DC I/4-0-6; data on the policy by American Zionists of "playing fair" within the Sterling Bloc and not obtaining more sterling for their dollars are in Folders DC I/1-6-4/10; and letters requesting information about goods permissible for import from the United States are in Folders DC I/4-0-6/2; DC I/4-50-0/2.

Collection cataloged by repository.

Research access not restricted. Photocopies provided.

DF 2/82

MANDATORY GOVERNMENT, DEPARTMENT OF HEALTH

Ca. 6 items, covering years 1925-1946, in Record Group 10. In Israel State Archives, Jerusalem.

The collection includes letters and reports concerning American Zion Commonwealth involvement in Afula: town planning, housing repairs, sewerage and drainage (Folder 6112/1660N).

Collection cataloged by repository.

Research access not restricted. Photocopies provided.

DR 11/81

MANDATORY GOVERNMENT, DEPARTMENT OF LABOUR

Ca. 115 items, covering years 1942-1947, in Record Group 13. In Israel State Archives, Jerusalem.

The collection contains letters and memos concerning visits of Labour Department inspectors reviewing safety facilities and provisions on the premises of the American Dress Company, the American Porcelain Tooth Company and the AMAL Mechanical Workshop and Printing Press. Also included are accident reports of their employees (Folders AMER 13-1429, PORC 13-1429, AMAL 13-1429); matters relating to labor disputes and their settlement at the American Porcelain Tooth Co. (PORC 13-1429); and the visit to the American representative of the delegation of the World Federation of Trade Unions (CL/179#10).

Collection cataloged by repository.

Research access not restricted. Photocopies provided.

HK 3/82

MANDATORY GOVERNMENT, DEPARTMENT OF MIGRATION (1920-1948)

Ca. 85 items, covering years 1923-1935, in Record Group 11. In Israel State Archives, Jerusalem.

The collection contains letters, memoranda, reports and press extracts regarding American involvement in business, agriculture, construction, labor and finances in Eretz Yisrael. Among the items are requests by Economic Committee (AEC) for Palestine addressed to the Immigration Department for statistics of agricultural crops in 1934 (The American Folder 1227/14); a list of "capitalistic immigrants" who entered Palestine 1932-1934 (request refused) (Folder 1226/23), as well as the AEC's sending the Immigration Department copies of *Palestine Economic News* (Folder 1227/1); earnings, production, etc. of the American Auto Company, among those listed in a 1935 report by the Labour Department of the Jewish Agency (Folder 1227/31); visits in 1927 of American businessmen and of James F. Hodgson, Commercial Attaché of the American Legation in Egypt, the latter to assemble material for an economic development study (Folder 1223/20); acquisition of a concrete mixing machine from American-Jewish trade unions, road construction by Solel Boneh for the American Zion Commonwealth and the possibility of loans from American banks for construction in towns and agricultural settlements (Folder 1158/28).

Of special interest is the correspondence relating to alleged irregularities and fraud by the American Palestine Bank and its owner Samuel Benjamin, an American citizen, in 1925-1927. The correspondence focuses on the legal investigation of the bank and on the refusal by the Immigration Department to allow its inclusion on the list of guarantor banks for immigrants/travelers.

Collection cataloged by repository.

Research access not restricted. Photocopies provided.

HK 1/82

MANDATORY GOVERNMENT, DIRECTOR OF CUSTOMS AND EXCISE (DCE)

Ca. 465 items, covering years 1926-1948, in Record Group 128.

In Israel State Archives, Jerusalem.

The collection contains letters, forms, lists, invoices, vouchers and circulars concerning the exemptions and collections of customs duty, as well as other miscellaneous matters pertaining to the shipments of goods from the United States or matters relating to the United States and the Customs and Excise Department. Included are requests for exemptions from customs and refunds of import duty for a wide variety of merchandise, submitted to the DCE by the following institutions: American Friends Mission, Ramallah, for laboratory chemicals, etc. (Folder 221/26); American Economic Committee for Palestine for poultry, films (Folder 1161/47); Harry Fischel Institute, New York branch, requesting building materials from USA (Folder 329/47); Women's Zionist Organization for worn clothing from New York (Folder 210/26); American Consulate General for personal belongings of its personnel (Folder 284/26); Mizrachi Ladies' Organization for clothing, sewing machines (Folder 208/26); the American Colony Stores for 150,000 sheets of cut cellophane (Folder 2571/34); BOAC on behalf of Pan Am Airways and U.S. Army Air Corps for oil and a car engine (Folder 249/42); Oriental Institute of the University of Chicago and Megiddo Expedition for motor car, cameras and carpets (Folder 651/27).

There is also information on the collection of duty by the DCE from the Jaffa Company, which bought lime squash from the American sale of the American factory at Tel Litwinsky (Folder 1941/43); correspondence regarding consideration by the U.S. Alcohol Control Administration of regulations for the labeling of wines, and a request by the Department of Agriculture and Forests for information about the amount of wine exported to the United States (Folder 441/34); a list of "The Principle Articles Consigned Direct From USA in 1931," including cars, wheat, flour, tires, tubes (Folder 420/32); requests from the American Consulate for information regarding the shipments of merchandise to the United States (Folder 1044/43; 1238/42); a secret report of DCE to the Chief Secretary indicating no economic penetration of Palestine by the United States (Folder 508/46); a statement by the British Secretary of State for Foreign Affairs to the British Ambassador in Washington, D.C. that the Palestine Economic Bureau is exclusively Jewish, and the impression should not be given that it has official status (Folder 2758/34); DCE lists of steamers due at ports of Eretz Yisrael issued by the American Express Co. in 1928-1930 (Folder 2490/27); and an inquiry by the *Chicago Tribune* whether the Palestine government wishes to advertise in its supplement devoted to Jewish accomplishments in Eretz Yisrael (Folder 806/34).

Collection cataloged by repository.

Research access not restricted. Photocopies provided.

DF 5/82

MANDATORY GOVERNMENT, ECONOMIC ADVISER
3 items, dated 1943, in Record Group 5.
In Israel State Archives, Jerusalem.

The items consist of correspondence between Julius Simon (president of the Palestine Economic Corporation in America) and Geoffrey Walsh, economic adviser and chairman of the General Agricultural Council in Eretz Yisrael, discussing U.S. Department of Agriculture specifications for citrus juices of potential importance for citrus export (Folder 1463/N).
Collection cataloged by repository.
Research access not restricted. Photocopies provided.

HK 7/81

MANDATORY GOVERNMENT, PUBLIC WORKS DEPARTMENT
Ca. 34 items, covering the years 1924-1926, in Record Group 12.
In Israel State Archives, Jerusalem.

Collection contains correspondence between the American Zion Commonwealth and the Public Works Department concerning the former's offer of financing most of the construction of a Haifa-Afula road (Box 4105).
Collection cataloged by repository.
Research access not restricted. Photocopies provided.

DF 1/82

MANDATORY GOVERNMENT, WAR SUPPLY BOARD
Ca. 5½ linear feet, covering years 1942-1947, in Record Group 18.
In Israel State Archives, Jerusalem.

The collection contains letters, telegrams, invoices, financial accounts, bills of lading, circulars, memoranda and certificates of insurance concerning the following subjects: the supply, shipment, insurance, storage and cost of goods sent to Eretz Yisrael from the United States under the Lend-Lease Act (Folders 2-9/2-2; 2-9/3-5; 2-9/6-1; 4-0-2/18, 43,44,47-49, 58-59; 4-0-12/1 (Volumes 1 & 11), 2-4; 4-0-13; 4-0-17; 4-0-21/11; 4-0-40/46, 68-216; 4-0-41/79-110; 4-0-53/3, 14; 4-0-56/1-6; 4-0-57/2; 4-1/20-1; 4-2/1-52; 4-3-0/1-2);

disagreements within British ministries on matters concerning the shipment of lend-lease goods from Egypt to Palestine (Folder 4-0-2/50); offer by a company in New Jersey to sell radio masts and towers to the War Supply Board (Folder 4-0-2/56); complaint about the inundation by American agricultural equipment and a call to increase the export of agricultural machinery to Eretz Yisrael from British manufacturers (Folder 4-3-0 Volume IV 1a); administrative arrangements for the diversion to the Sudan of agricultural machinery from the United States destined for Eretz Yisrael (Folder 4-3-0/7); a resolution by the Palestine Association of Commission Agents that firms in the United States should not be prevented from exporting goods to Eretz Yisrael and that Britain should seek to protect agents representing those firms in Eretz Yisrael from losing their commissions on those supplies (Folder 4-0-2/22); and opposition by the Controller of Foreign Exchange of the Mandatory Government to importation of Egyptian stocks of commodities originating in the United States (Folder 4-0-6/4).
Collection cataloged by repository.
Research access not restricted. Photocopies provided.

DF 3/82

MARSHALL, LOUIS, 1856-1929
(U.S. lawyer and prominent Jewish communal leader; president of American Jewish Committee, 1912-1929.)
1 folder, covering years 1923-1925.
In Zionist Archives and Library, New York City.
    Contains correspondence dealing with American Jewish involvement in the Palestine Investment Corporation and the organizing of non-Zionists as members of the Jewish Agency.   Includes also a pamphlet entitled *American Jewry and the Rebuilding of Palestine*. Material not cataloged by repository.
Research access not restricted. Photocopies provided.

RM 1/75

MEROM (MEREMINSKI), ISRAEL, 1891-1976
(Born in Slonim, Poland; active in Zionist circles; emigrated to Eretz Yisrael in 1924; Histadrut emissary for campaigns among Jewish labor groups in the United States in 1928, 1929, 1931 and

1932-1933; Histadrut representative in America 1939-1945.) 6 boxes, covering years 1928-1933 and 1939-1945, in private papers of Israel Merom.
In Hakibbutz Hameuhad Archives, Ramat Ef'al, Ramat Gan.

Collection includes personal working notes, correspondence, reports, contracts and financial reports, minutes of meetings and other documents pertaining to Merom's activities in the United States on behalf of the Histadrut, mainly concerning American relations with commercial companies and economic investment in Eretz Yisrael.

Some of the subjects discussed are:

stimulating American interest in the Yachin Company;
prices of equipment from America for the "Fenitzia" glass factory;
correspondence and negotiations regarding the establishment of a Jewish shipping company, including a memorandum written by Merom on the establishment of the Palestine Freight Maritime Company (1943?);
purchase of meat in the United States by Hamashbir Hamerkazi;
distribution of Bank Hapoalim shares in the United States;
contracts of Solel Boneh and Koor with American companies involved in economic projects in Eretz Yisrael and the east; and
activities of Ampal, Amco, the Palestine Economic Corporation and the Palestine Economic Committee in land purchase, fund raising and investment.

Collection not cataloged.
Research access not restricted. Photocopies provided.

TG 9/81

MODZOFF, CHUNA
1 item, dated 1946, in Louis Marshall Collection.
In Zionist Archives and Library, New York City.

Contains the 4th Annual Report of the American Palestine Trading Corporation for 1946.
Material not cataloged by repository.
Research access not restricted. Photocopies provided.

RM 1/75

NADAV (HALPERN), ZVI, 1891-1959
(Engineer; one of the founders of Hashomer; early settler of Degania and Merhavia.)
2 items, dated 1944 and 1945, in Record Group 5/1.
In Yad Yitzhak Ben Zvi, Jerusalem.
   The items are a bulletin (August, 1944) and minutes of a meeting (May 8, 1945) in Hebrew of Palabrus, an organization that promoted trade between Palestine, Great Britain, the USSR and the United States (Folder 5/1/3/11).
Collection classified by repository.
Research access not restricted. Photocopies provided.

AF 4/82

NEUMANN, EMANUEL, 1893-1980
(Active American Zionist leader, cofounder of Keren Hayesod in the United States; member of the Jewish Agency Executive in Jerusalem, 1931-1941.)
Ca. 80 items, covering years 1929-1933, interspersed in Record Group A123.
In Central Zionist Archives, Jerusalem.
   The development of Tiberias as a health spa is dealt with in Folders 25 and 26. Of special interest in the latter are tables and architects' plans to implement this suggestion.
   Folder 34 contains letters (July 6, 1933) about the Levant Fair, the need for the American Palestine Investment Corporation and land purchases in Transjordan and Ghor Kybr. Folder 18 deals with the American Zion Commonwealth and Herzliya.
Material cataloged by repository.
Research access not restricted. Photocopies provided.

TzB 11/74

ORGANIZATION OF JERUSALEM MERCHANTS
(Established 1935 by small businessmen and manufacturers.)
10 items, covering years 1934-1948, interspersed in M4 G1/206.
In Jerusalem Municipality-Historical Archives, Jerusalem.
   The collection consists of business correspondence, among which is a letter from Kurt Gruenwald of the American Economic Committee for Palestine (January 2, 1944) about the interest of

U.S. manufacturers in the industrial development of Palestine.
Material not cataloged by repository.
Research access not restricted. Photocopies provided.

RB 9/74

PALESTINE COOPERATIVE COMPANY, INC.
2 items, covering years 1922-1924.
In Zionist Archives and Library, New York City.
    Contains a brochure explaining its investment activities and a financial statement for May, 1924.
Material not cataloged by repository.
Research access not restricted. Photocopies provided.

RM 6/73

PALESTINE DEVELOPMENT COUNCIL
(Established 1921.)
1 large folder, covering years 1923-1925, in Julian W. Mack Papers (XII 42a).
In Zionist Archives and Library, New York City.
    Contains memoranda, reports of meetings, letters, etc. concerning the following matters: the "development of the Kvuzoth into true, self-supporting cooperatives"; the development of new colonies; the granting of loans to various agricultural projects (Pardes Orange Growers Cooperative Society, Almond Growers Cooperative Society, Palestine Tobacco Growers Association, etc.); an interview with Sir Herbert Samuel regarding oil interests and the future of Arab rule in the Middle East; arrangements with Baron Edmond de Rothschild on financing various projects; the Rutenberg Project; Max Manischewitz's plans to open matzoh, noodle and macaroni factories and a kosher hotel in Jerusalem; development of oil, gas and mineral ventures (Rothschild objected to oil exploration in northern Palestine on religious grounds); and the establishment of Palestine Development Leagues throughout the United States in association with PDC.
    Contains also an extensive diary of Jacob De Haas's activities in Palestine and of the political and economic situation of the time (reporting several meetings with American Jews in Palestine in which unfair treatment toward them was expressed), covering the period September 14, 1924 to February 27, 1925. Includes correspondence

from Judge Julian Mack giving detailed descriptions and impressions of his trip through Palestine (1923). Other correspondents include De Haas, F. Julius Fohs, Benjamin Cohen, Julius Simon and Robert Szold.

Material cataloged by repository.

Research access not restricted. Photocopies provided.

RM 1/75

PALESTINE DEVELOPMENT LEAGUE

1 folder, covering years 1921-1923.

In Zionist Archives and Library, New York City.

Contains the minutes (1921-1923) and the Constitution, which states as the group's purpose aiding in the "social economic upbuilding of Palestine so that it may be populated within a comparatively short time, by a preponderating body of manly, self-supporting Jews endowed with the highest Jewish ideals and fitted to become citizens of a self-governing commonwealth."

Material not cataloged by repository.

Research access not restricted. Photocopies provided.

RM 6/73

PALESTINE ECONOMIC CORPORATION

4 large folders, covering years 1922-1948, interspersed in Robert Szold Papers (VI-4).

In Zionist Archives and Library, New York City.

The objective of the PEC was to "give material aid on a strictly business basis to productive Palestinian enterprises and thereby further the economic development of the Holy Land and the resettlement of an increasing number of Jews." The collection contains correspondence concerning the 80th birthday celebration for Brandeis in which was discussed a "suitable commemoration" project in Palestine, which resulted in the purchase of additional land adjoining the American colony at Ein Hashofet as a "Sister Colony."

Includes also correspondence of Robert Szold, Stephen S. Wise, Moshe Shertok, Chaim Weizmann and Louis D. Brandeis concerning the advisability and contents of a memo to be submitted in the name of American Jewry to the Peel Commission, established in 1936 to investigate the "legitimate grievances" among Arabs and Jews in

Palestine, the legal positions of the opposing parties, and the liabilities for riot damages. One letter states, "Whether or not 'an American case' will eventually be presented the claims and grievances of the American Jews with respect to Palestine should be formulated now and made public as soon as possible."

Contains also an account of the political exchange between the United States and Great Britain regarding "interest of the United States in the establishment of the Jewish National Homeland in Palestine," and a 1936 Economic Research Institute report on "Jewish Colonization in Palestine."

Published materials include an article by Julius Simon, *Policy and Activities of the PEC of New York*; the prospectus, president's report for 1922, a pamphlet—*Investment in Palestine*—of the Palestine Cooperative Company, Inc. and an article "Expansion of Palestine Corporation."

Material cataloged by repository.

Research access not restricted. Photocopies provided.

RM 1/75

PALESTINE ENDOWMENT FUNDS, INC.

1.   1 box, covering years 1922-1941, in Robert Szold Papers (IV 1-10).

In Zionist Archives and Library, New York City.

Contains the correspondence concerning raising and distributing contributions for such projects as the Hebrew University, Bezalel Art School (classes, museum and library), a home for Yemenite children, the Education Association of Jerusalem (Deborah Kallen's school), Palestine Potash Ltd., a proposal and patents for equipment to extract oil and quicklime from bituminous limestone, support of a student studying aviation, Histadruth-Yakin, Kibbutz America of the Hashomer Hatzair, Central Kupath Milveh Association, the Institute of Palestine Natural History and Brandeis's contributions toward a settlement of the Gulf of Akaba and the transference of funds to David Ben-Gurion for use by the Jewish Agency.

Correspondents include Julian Mack, Jacob De Haas, Henrietta Szold, Robert Szold, Isaac Hamlin (National Labor Committee for the Jewish workers in Palestine), Louis D. Brandeis, David Ben-Gurion and Felix Warburg.

Includes also a listing of shares in the Jewish Colonial Trust held by the PEF (February, 1934), a statement of "Palestinian Investments and Other Assets of 12/31/36" with comments, the accounts held with the Anglo-Palestine Company Ltd. (1926-1927) for various projects, the "Trust Funds for the Benefit of the Hebrew University" for 1925 (specifically the Department of Jewish Studies, Hebrew Department, Medical Department and Jerusalem Library) and various publications promoting the work of the PEF.

Includes also correspondence from Teddy Kollek, Stephen S. Wise and Julian Mack concerning the naming of the Ein Gev Settlement for Mack, and the misunderstanding that arose over it with the Jewish National Fund.

Material cataloged by repository.

Research access not restricted. Photocopies provided.

RM 1/75

2.   8 items, covering years 1922-1948.

In Zionist Archives and Library, New York City.

Includes certificate of incorporation and pamphlet describing it as a corporation "empowered to accept gifts and bequests" to support religious and educational endeavors in Palestine. Contains also the annual auditor's reports for 1923-1948, minutes of the Board of Trustees for 1922-1924, 1926, 1928 and 1930-1948 and a copy of the By-Laws of the organization.

Material not cataloged by repository.

Research access not restricted. Photocopies provided.

RM 6/73

PALESTINE EXHIBITS, INC.

2 boxes, covering years 1937-1940.

In Zionist Archives and Library, New York City.

Contains the minutes (6/37-10/40) covering the discussion of a proposed exhibit at the 1939 New York World's Fair to demonstrate to the world and to the Jews of America the work of the Jews in Palestine, the period of the exhibit, and its "liquidation."

Includes also financial statements for 1938-1940, lists of exhibits, and correspondence relating to them.

Material not cataloged by repository.

Research access not restricted. Photocopies provided.

RM 6/73

PALESTINE OFFICE, JAFFA (TEL AVIV) AND JERUSALEM

(Established in 1908 by the World Zionist Organization; served as the central agency in Palestine for settlement activities including land purchase and aid to immigration during the Ottoman period; absorbed in 1919 by the Zionist Commission.)

Ca. 3 inches, covering years 1908-1919, interspersed and in special folders in Record Group L2.

In Central Zionist Archives, Jerusalem.

The collection contains extensive correspondence (1914-1915) about the sale of Bezalel products in the United States as well as loans for Bezalel (Folders 87/VII, 87/VIII). There is also correspondence about loans to orange growers, the sale of oranges in the United States and the import of urgently needed petroleum from the United States (Folder 104).

Several letters from Mrs. Sarah Thon about importing lace from Palestine are found in Folder 249/II. The suggestion that shares of the Palestine Land Development Company should be sold for investment purposes is found in Folder 2/IX. A request for information about the possibility of starting a tobacco industry is noted in Folder 20, and lists of recipients of money from the Palestine Economic Corporation are located in Folders 235/I and 235/II.

Material cataloged by repository.

Research access not restricted. Photocopies provided.

OZ 3/75

PALESTINE SAVINGS AND INVESTMENT CORPORATION OF THE BRONX

1 item, undated.

In Zionist Archives and Library, New York City.

Contains a notice of a meeting as part of a membership drive to increase the number of Bronx Zionists participating in their program.

Material not cataloged by repository.
Research access not restricted. Photocopies provided.

RM 6/73

PALESTINE SECURITIES, INC.
1 box, covering years 1923-1929.
In Zionist Archives and Library, New York City.

Contains the certificate of incorporation signed by Jacob Massel, Bernard A. Rosenblatt and Louis J. Rosenblatt, wherein the purpose of the group is stated: "To manufacture, export, import, buy, sell and generally deal in goods, wares, merchandise and property, of every class and description; to . . . dispose of letters of patent of the United States or any foreign country . . . to purchase, lease or otherwise acquire all kinds of personal property . . . securities . . . to borrow money, make and issue promissory notes . . . to carry on a general shipping and forwarding business . . . . " Also contains the minutes of meetings (1923-1927) concerning their business dealings, financial statements (1926-1928) and correspondence (1926-1929).
Material not cataloged by repository.
Research access not restricted. Photocopies provided.

RM 6/73

PEOPLE'S RELIEF COMMITTEE
(Established August, 1915, representing labor element of the American Jewish community, to collect funds for Jewish war sufferers in Europe; in November, 1915 became one of three separate commissions in Joint Distribution Committee.)
4 items, covering years 1920-1923, in Box 4 of collection (I-13).
In American Jewish Historical Society, Waltham, Massachusetts.

Contains an undated memorandum and some correspondence regarding construction work in Palestine to be financed by the Workmen's Bank and the Reconstruction Committee of the Joint Distribution Committee, as well as a letter to P. Rutenberg requesting information relative to the progress of his electrification scheme (August 23, 1923).

Collection cataloged by repository.
Research access not restricted. Photocopies provided.

JDS 6/75

QUARRIES
2 items, undated.
In Zionist Archives and Library, New York City.

Contains an 11-page report on the feasibility of investing in quarry operations in Palestine and the resolution forming the Organizing Committee of the investment group, among whose members were Harry Fischel and Jacob De Haas.
Material not cataloged by repository.
Research access not restricted. Photocopies provided.

RM 6/73

ROKACH, ISAAC, 1894-1974
(Active in business affairs connected with the citrus industry in Palestine; director of the Pardess Syndicate of Palestine Citrus Growers, 1927; editor of *Hadar*, citrus monthly.)
Ca. 10 items, dated 1931-1947, in Record Group A323.
In Central Zionist Archives, Jerusalem.

The collection includes contracts, letters and engineering sketches by the Knappen Engineering Company in New York regarding a construction project in the Tel Aviv harbor in 1948 (Folder 149); correspondence regarding commercial ties between Etz Hazait and the Gershoni Company, New York, for olive oil export (Folder 17); correspondence regarding purchase of American crates for citrus packing, 1946-1947 (Folders 120/3; 127/2); correspondence with Rokach representing the interests in Palestine of the American families Lamport, Ezra & Sylvia Shapiro and Katz in a landownership dispute, information on the price of land in Herzliya and the use of a blocked bank account in 1947 (Folders 121/2; 127/2).
Collection cataloged by repository.
Research access not restricted. Photocopies provided.

SG 11/81

RUPPIN, ARTHUR, 1876-1943
(Father of Zionist settlement in Eretz Yisrael; b. Germany; settled in Eretz Yisrael before World War I; economist and sociologist.)
11 items, dated 1922, in Folder 258 in Record Group S55.
In Central Zionist Archives, Jerusalem.
     Collection includes correspondence, mostly between Arthur Ruppin and Louis Lipsky regarding financing mortgages, acquiring land and establishing a credit union in Eretz Yisrael.
Collection cataloged by repository.
Research access not restricted. Photocopies provided.

DF 11/81

RUTENBERG CONCESSION
1 box, dated 1922.
In Zionist Archives and Library, New York City.
     Includes the plans for using the Rivers Jordan and Yarmuk for making electric power, a digest of the concession made by the British Government to Pinhas Rutenberg, an analysis of the plans and a record of available assets, all collected by the Palestine Economic Corporation to study for possible involvement in the project.
Material not cataloged by repository.
Research access not restricted. Photocopies provided.

RM 6/73

SACHER, HARRY, 1881-1971
(Active British Zionist, lawyer, author and journalist; member of Zionist Executive, 1927-1931.)
5 items, covering years 1944-1945, in Record Group A289.
In Central Zionist Archives, Jerusalem.
     The items consist of manuscripts for newspaper articles and a letter and a prospectus dealing with the industrial development of Eretz Yisrael and the Palestine Economic Corporation. Material on the adaptation of American industrial methods to increase productivity in labor and quality of products and the recruitment of Anglo-American administrative and commercial talents for Eretz Yisrael is found in Folders 62, 66, 101. A 4-page proposal sent by Moshe Novomeysky to Sacher dated September 14, 1945,

suggesting the establishment of an Industrial Research Foundation to promote industrial development in Eretz Yisrael and an advisory committee to adapt American methods and discoveries made during World War II is in Folder 62. The American Economic Corporation is cited as an example of a successful, nonphilanthropic industrial enterprise in 1945 (Folder 101).

Of special interest is a 6-page printed prospectus of the Palestine Economic Corporation, describing its development, operation, principal assets and subsidiaries. Photographs, a list of the board of directors and the 1925 prospectus are included (Folder 101).

Collection cataloged by repository.

Research access not restricted. Photocopies provided.

SH 6/81

SHARNOPOLSKY, SAMUEL, 1918-1943
(Born in Ukraine; immigrated to Palestine, 1927; promoted idea of health resorts and other investments in Eretz Yisrael; organized Palestine exhibits at World Fairs in Chicago, 1933-1934 and in New York, 1934 and 1939).

Ca. ½ inch, covering years 1933-1938, in Record Group A318. In Central Zionist Archives, Jerusalem.

Folder 3 of the collection includes letters of introduction to prominent American Jews, brochures with photographs, personal travel documents and newspaper clippings regarding efforts by Sharnopolsky to develop Eretz Yisrael as a health resort and tourist center and as a center for business, industrial and agricultural investments through exhibits at World Fairs in Chicago (1933-1934) and New York (1934 and 1939) and the Palestine Exhibition in New York, 1936-1937.

Among the prominent persons and institutions mentioned are Morris Rothenberg, Senator Royal S. Copeland, B. Manischewitz, Palestine Government Railways, the Amalgamated Bank of New York, the Zionist Organization of Chicago and the American Economic Committee for Palestine.

Collection cataloged by repository.

Research access not restricted. Photocopies provided.

SH 6/81

SZOLD, HENRIETTA (THE JEWISH AGENCY, OFFICES OF
THE MEMBERS OF THE EXECUTIVE, 1928-1930)
4 items, dated 1928, in Folder 15 in Record Group S48.
In Central Zionist Archives, Jerusalem.

The material concerns a suggestion to carry out experiments
on oranges that had been developed in California in the Experi-
mental Station in Palestine.
Collection cataloged by repository.
Research access not restricted. Photocopies provided.

OZ 11/75

TULIN, ABRAHAM, 1882-1973
(American Zionist; delegate to Zionist congresses; member of
Executive Committee, ZOA; member of American Zionist Emer-
gency Council; chief counsel for American Zionist organizations
before Anglo-American Committee of Inquiry on the Palestine
Question.)
Ca. 147 items, covering years 1921-1930, in Record Group A342.
In Central Zionist Archives, Jerusalem.

The collection includes correspondence, reports, minutes of
meetings, diary entries and stock prospectus relating to the Rutenberg Hydro-Electric Project, the Dead Sea Concession contacts with
key figures in the American oil industry, and the Palestine Economic
Corporation:

1. Rutenberg Hydro-Electric Project (Folders 1-5;7-10;59):
The material describes the negotiations between British and American
Jews and administrative details in the years 1921-1923 concerning
the establishment of a capital stock company to finance the
Rutenberg Hydro-Electric Project; activities of the Palestine Develop-
ment Council, the Palestine Cooperative Company, and the Economic
Board for Palestine; and a scientific evaluation of the project by an
American expert.

Correspondents and participants figuring prominently include
Pinhas Rutenberg, Abraham Tulin, Julian W. Mack, Irving Lehman,
Louis D. Brandeis, Irma Lindheim, Felix M. Warburg, Robert Szold,
Julius Simon, Horace Kallen, Bernard Flexner, Samuel Rosensohn,
Herbert Lehman, Jacob De Haas, Louis Lowenstein (consulting
engineer for General Electric who expressed his professional opinion

of the project), Ben Cohen, James de Rothschild and Sir Robert Waley Cohen. Organizations mentioned in connection with the project include the Central Conference of American Rabbis and the Zionist Organization of America.

Of special interest is a 32-page prospectus (July, 1922) of the project issued by the Palestine Development Council for the sale and subscription of preferred and common shares in the company (Folder 3).

2. Dead Sea Concession (Folders 12, 13, 15, 16, 19, 24, 25 and 83): The material describes American involvement from 1925-1930 in the negotiations between Moshe Novomeysky (with his partner Major Tulloch) and the British Government in his attempts to obtain a concession for extracting potash, bromine, etc. from the waters of the Dead Sea; administrative details of financing the concession through the sale of shares by the Palestine Development Council and Palestine Cooperative Company to American investors; chemical and economic evaluations of the concession by American experts; and early attempts to rally support for the concession in America.

Correspondents and participants figuring prominently, besides Tulin and Novomeysky, are Julian Mack, Louis D. Brandeis, Robert Szold, Israel B. Brodie, Herbert Lehman, Bernard Flexner, Julius Simon, Sol Rosensohn, Isadore L. Lubin (economic expert) and L. L. Summers and Co. (chemists consulted). Organizations and enterprises involved include the Palestine Development Council, the Palestine Cooperative Co. Inc., the Palestine Mining Syndicate Ltd. and Palestine Potash Ltd.

Of special interest are the following:

2a. a letter (November 21, 1928) to Brandeis from Tulin, enclosing a letter from Novomeysky discussing the importance of Jewish control of the Dead Sea Concession "not only from a Jewish but also from the American point of view" because of the dependence of America on the German Potash Syndicate. "Should we be in control of the Concession, America would be our principal market to the mutual profit of both America and the Jewish National Home" (Folder 12).

2b. Handwritten note (December 21, 1928) from Brandeis, sending Tulin the address of Isadore L. Lubin, an economist with the Brookings Institution, whom Brandeis had suggested to study the economic features of the proposed exploitation of Dead Sea minerals (Folder 12).

2c. List (November 1, 1935) of Jewish and non-Jewish subscribers of the Palestine Potash Ltd.

3. Jewish Agency contacts with key figures in the American oil industry include the petroleum attaché of the State Department. Of special interest is a letter (May 23, 1945) from William Fondiller, president of the American Society for the Technion, to Tulin concerning the suggestion of Dr. Lester Goldsmith, chief engineer of Atlantic Refining Co., Philadelphia, to contact John Leavell, petroleum attaché for the Middle East of the State Department. Fondiller recommended that Tulin approach Leavell through the Jewish Agency. Other possible connections mentioned were Michael Halpern, vice-chairman in charge of refining, and Starr Rogers, chairman of the board, both of Texas Oil Co. (Folder 39).

4. Palestine Economic Corporation: The material describes the views of Louis D. Brandeis on colonization and economic developments within the *Yishuv*, 1929-1930 (Folder 61).

Collection cataloged by repository.

Research access not restricted.   Photocopies provided.

SH 5/82

UNITED STATES, OFFICE OF STRATEGIC SERVICES
3 items, covering years 1942-1945, interspersed in Record Group 226. In United States National Archives and Records Service, Washington, D.C.

There are approximately 5 inches of documents in the Economic Section, of which 3 items pertain to America and the Holy Land. The documents provide economic background material through annual, quarterly and monthly economic and financial reports, surveys of industry and agriculture and transportation and communication facilities; data on immigration and national income; and studies of development potential in the Negev, water resources and absorptive capacity, in terms of immigration after the war. The effects of the war on the economy of Palestine and postwar reconstruction plans are also included in this section. The Arab-Jewish conflict is reflected through complaints that the British favor Arab produce and the refusal of Jews to participate in post-war economic planning because of the White Paper.

The few items directly relevant include *An Annual Economic and Financial Review, 1942*, prepared by A. E. Lippencott; a report that James B. Hays, formerly employed by the TVA, has been hired by the Zionists to develop plans for a large-scale irrigation system starting at the Syrian border and extending to the Negev; and one minor item that refers to the British control of the sale of auto parts that excludes any opportunity for Palestinians to purchase these items from the United States.

Collection cataloged by repository.

Research access restricted to declassified documents. Photocopies provided.

JT 1/76

WISE, STEPHEN SAMUEL, 1874-1949
(Internationally prominent American rabbi, communal figure, and Zionist leader.)
Ca. 200 items, covering years 1914-1948, interspersed in collection (P-134).
In American Jewish Historical Society, Waltham, Massachusetts.

The collection contains miscellaneous minutes and correspondence (1921-1935) relating to the Palestine Development Council and PDC leagues (Box 129:4), as well as scattered references to these organizations found in the correspondence of Jacob De Haas (Box 107:22), Abba Hillel Silver (Box 119:20) and Robert Szold (Box 120:13).

The Emanuel Neumann correspondence (Box 128:8) includes material on the Palestine Economic Corporation, specifically with reference to the Transjordanian project (1931-) for the development of Transjordan by settlement of German refugees and infusion of U.S. capital. Arab leaders and Louis D. Brandeis expressed interest in the scheme (Box 106:3, June 26, 1933). Neumann was also involved in the Industrial and Financial Corporation of Palestine (1934), designed to actively promote "the investment of private capital in constructive enterprise on business lines."

Other facets of the economic relations between the United States and the Holy Land that are reflected in the collection are (in chronological order) a 1914 scheme to increase the imports of Holy Land goods to the United States (Box 130:14, Pewsner to Magnes, December 11, 1914); E. Z. Lewin-Epstein's attempt (1915-1916) to increase the sale and distribution of Carmel wines in America (Box 113:10); the Dvir Corporation's 1928 sale of stocks and books in the United States (Box 126:10); correspondence (especially with Thomas H. Norton) and reports regarding the 1927 sale of concessions to exploit Dead Sea resources (Box 100:5); the sale of Palestine products throughout the United States (Box 129:7); the Palestine Investors Service (New York), Bulletin #1 (January 24, 1932), entitled "Present Opportunities in Palestine Orange Growing Industry" (Box 106:3); "Notes of a conversation with Mr. Johnson the Treasurer with Prof. Frankfurter on April 13, 1934" regarding the economic situation in Palestine and the Mid-East; Louis Brandeis's $20,000 investment in the 1935 Akaba project (Box 106: October 10, 1935); the circular letter of the Palestine Land Development Corporation (1938) set up "to increase the use of Tozeret Haaretz in America" (Box 129:8); the January 4, 1939 memo of Moshe de Shalit to Brandeis and Wise regarding the development of Herzliya (Box 106:7); and the 1945 correspondence with M. Feldschreiber regarding the Lowdermilk plan for Negev development via diversion of Jordan River waters (Box 108:10).

The Histadrut (Labor Palestine) committee literature and correspondence (1936-1948) also shed some light on the relationship between American and Palestinian workers (Box 128:3).

Material cataloged by repository.

Research access not restricted. Photocopies provided.

JDS 6/75

WOLF, HYMAN S.

(Editor of *Jewish Courier* and *Chicago Weekly*; first secretary of Order Knights of Zion of Chicago, founded in 1899.)

1 folder, covering years 1898-1944.

In Zionist Archives and Library, New York City.

Contains correspondence from the Order Knights of Zion and the Zion Association of Chicago, and from the Jerusalem Printing Works Association, a group of stockholders who founded the Printing Works. Contains also two certificates of membership from

the Order Knights of Zion dated 1899. Seeking Christian support for Zionism, Wolf's letter to Rev. Thomas Crane elicited the following reply: "I approve the sentiment but doubt the feasibility of the plan."
Material not cataloged by repository.
Research access not restricted. Photocopies provided.

RM 1/75

YOUNG MACCABEAN SOCIETY, DETROIT
2 items, dated 1918.
In Zionist Archives and Library, New York City.

Contains two letters concerning the purchase of stock by this Detroit group from the Jewish Colonial Trust, Ltd. (London) through the agency of the ZOA.
Material not cataloged by repository.
Research access not restricted. Photocopies provided.

RM 6/73

ZIONIST COMMISSION, JERUSALEM
(Organized in early 1918, consisting of representatives of several Western Zionist organizations to serve as liaison between the British military authority and the Jewish population in Palestine; assumed political functions of the Palestine Office of the World Zionist Organization, fully merging with it in the fall of 1919; superseded in 1921 by the Palestine Zionist Executive.)
Ca. 230 items, covering years 1913-1921, interspersed in special folders in Record Group L3.
In Central Zionist Archives, Jerusalem.

The bulk of the collection concerns itself with the Nathan Straus mother-of-pearl factory, which was at first a jewelry and other ornaments factory and later exclusively a button factory. There is much correspondence about the dispute between Dr. Levy, Straus's representative, and Yehudah Schneyor and Chanoch Dubno who "took over" the factory when Levy was exiled by the Turks (Folder 136a).

The collection also includes copies of a contract (1921) between Straus and Getsel Lusternik for the new "Zedefia" factory (Folders 133 and 136b) and letters from the Zionist Commission's Trade and

Industry Department (1919 and 1920) about marketing lace and tzitzith in the United States (Folders 38 I and 38 II.). Of interest is a letter from Dr. David de Sola Pool to Mayer M. Swaab, Jr., (August 31, 1919) about the dubious practicality of erecting a garbage incinerator in Jerusalem: "there is no Arabic word for 'incinerator,' and you can't buy something that has no name. The municipality here has its own conception of refuse disposal: it does not dispose of it, but allows the sun and time to do their relentless work" (Folder 38 I). Miscellaneous items in the collection can be found in Folders 83 XIII, 221 and 377.

Material cataloged by repository.

Research access not restricted. Photocopies provided.

OZ 2/75

ZIONIST ORGANIZATION, COPENHAGEN BUREAU (1914-1920)
10 items, covering years 1916-1917, interspersed in Record Group L6.

In Central Zionist Archives, Jerusalem.

Correspondence in Folders 12V, 12VI and 12VIII concerns the importation of ethrogim and lulavim to America from Palestine; permission to import Rishon le Zion wines and brandies for American Jews and having the U.S.S. *Des Moines* carry these wines; and orange loans. It also contains a letter (December 6, 1916) quoting Dr. Ruppin, "impressively warning against offering uncautiously land for sale." Two of the correspondents are Richard Lichtheim of the Copenhagen Bureau and Eliahu Lewin-Epstein on behalf of the Palestine Economic Corporation.

Material cataloged by repository.

Research access not restricted. Photocopies provided.

OZ 4/75

ZIONIST ORGANIZATION, THE JEWISH AGENCY FOR PALESTINE, CENTRAL OFFICE, LONDON
(The Central Office moved to London from Berlin after the 1920 London Conference.)
Ca. 15 items, covering the years 1921, 1924 and 1945, interspersed in Record Group Z4.

In Central Zionist Archives, Jerusalem.

Relevant items include copies of reports (1945) by James B. Hays, former project manager of TVA at Bristol, Tennessee, about irrigation and power possibilities in Palestine and the water supply of the Jordan River (Folder 14520). Folder 303/2 contains correspondence (1921) with William L. Jordan, interested "in the inauguration of steamship lines" in Palestine, a note suggesting the shipment of cotton to Palestine and a copy of a contract (April 25, 1921) between the American Fruit Growers of Palestine, Inc. and fruit growers of Rehovoth. Folder 2678 contains some correspondence (1924) concerning a Mr. Berditcheff who wanted to investigate the possibility of developing a sugar cane industry in Palestine.

Collection cataloged by repository.

Research access not restricted. Photocopies provided.

OZ 8/75

PART TWO
PHILANTHROPY

AGRON (AGRONSKY), GERSHON, 1893-1959

(Born in the Ukraine; moved to the United States in 1906; enlisted in Jewish Legion in 1918; resident of Palestine after demobilization except for 1921-1924; journalist and correspondent, founded and edited the *Palestine Post*; mayor of Jerusalem, 1955-1959).

9 items, covering years 1926-1927, interspersed in Record Group A209.

In Central Zionist Archives, Jerusalem.

Folder 15 contains correspondence (May 12, 1926-January 25, 1927) concerning the building of a central hospital for Emek Yizrael and the controversy between Kupat Holim and the American Zion Commonwealth about the building site. The hospital was to be built jointly by Hadassah and Kupat Holim.

The folder also contains a copy of a letter to B. G. Richards (February 11, 1926) taking to task Jacob Billikopf for donating $3.5 million to a Philadelphia building fund instead of to Palestine causes.

Material cataloged by repository.

Research access not restricted. Photocopies provided.

OZ 12/74

ALLIED JEWISH CAMPAIGN

Ca. 100 items, covering years 1929-1931, interspersed in 2 folders in Silver Archives (A Correspondence 4-1-6 to 4-1-7).

In The Temple, Cleveland, Ohio.

The collection contains correspondence concerning the 1929-1930 and 1930-1931 campaigns and Abba Hillel Silver's activities in Cleveland, Detroit, Youngstown, Des Moines, Louisville, Wheeling and Columbus. Of special interest are a letter from Ittamar Ben-Avi and Oved Ben-Ami of the Palestine Young Agriculturists Organization to Nathan Straus, thanking him for aid and describing the Jewish defense during the 1929 riots and the final financial report of the Emergency Fund for Palestine (4/18/1930).

Material not cataloged by repository.

Research access not restricted. Photocopies provided.

MF 1/75

AMERICAN BOARD OF COMMISSIONERS FOR FOREIGN MISSIONS

(Congregationalist missionary organization.)

35 items, covering years 1827-1920, interspersed in collection (ABC).

In Houghton Library, Harvard University, Cambridge, Massachusetts.

Consists of correspondence concerning the $100 contribution of Lewis Cass to Palestine missionaries in July, 1837 (ABC 16.8.2, Volume 1, item 310); the $31.66 collected in donations in 1841 (ibid., item 321); and the attempt by Rev. John Lannean to raise funds in Georgia for a Jerusalem chapel in 1841 (ABC 3.1, volume 298, pp. 183-184).

The bulk of the correspondence deals with World War I relief aid and the attempts to send rescue vessels to Jaffa (ABC 3.1, volume 298, pp. 183-184; ABC 3.2, volume 325, p. 351; volume 327, p. 244, 253 and 431-433; volume 328, pp. 37, 177, 223, 236, 282, 327, 535 and 547; volume 333, p. 635; volume 334, pp. 12, 25, 28, 140, 239 and 492; ABC 16.5, volume 6, pp. 206-208). In addition, the war-front relief activities of missionary Stephen Trowbridge in Palestine are detailed (ABC 3.1, volume 305, p. 400; volume 307, p. 481; ABC 16.9.3, volume 45, item 41) and there is correspondence regarding postwar charitable aid (1920) to the Armenian Patriarchate in Jerusalem (ABC 16.5, volume 8, pp. 13-14).

Table of contents prepared for each volume.

Research access not restricted. Photocopies provided.

JDS 7/75

AMERICAN COMMITTEE FOR CIVIL LIBERTIES IN PALESTINE

1 item, dated 1938, in Silver Archives (A correspondence 4-1-62).

In The Temple, Cleveland, Ohio.

Contains a letter from the Committee to Abba Hillel Silver soliciting financial aid.
Material not cataloged by repository.
Research access not restricted. Photocopies provided.

MF 1/75

AMERICAN COMMITTEE FOR THE NATIONAL SICK FUND OF PALESTINE, INC.
2 items, undated.
In Zionist Archives and Library, New York City.
Contains brochures used to raise funds for increasing the number of beds in Palestine hospitals.
Material not cataloged by repository.
Research access not restricted. Photocopies provided.

RM 6/73

AMERICAN COMMITTEE OF OSE, INC.
1 item, undated.
In Zionist Archives and Library, New York City.
Contains a membership promotion pamphlet, which states: "The OSE is the only world-wide Jewish organization which concerns itself with health problems of Jews everywhere."
Material not cataloged by repository.
Research access not restricted. Photocopies provided.

RM 6/73

AMERICAN FRIENDS OF THE HEBREW UNIVERSITY
1 box, dated 1931-1953.
In Zionist Archives and Library, New York City.
Contains news releases of the American Advisory Committee concerning the library, scientific research, etc.; a brochure on fund raising by the American Jewish Physicians' Committee for building the new medical school; various fund-raising materials; press releases; and the *Bulletin on the Hebrew University* (1938-1941).
Material not cataloged by repository.
Research access not restricted. Photocopies provided.

RM 6/73

AMERICAN FUND FOR PALESTINIAN INSTITUTIONS
1 folder, covering years 1942-1945.
In Zionist Archives and Library, New York City.
    Contains reports on the Fund's activities, pamphlets—one of which states that the Fund's purpose is to "coordinate the fund-raising activities of 69 Palestinian educational, cultural, and welfare institutions"—and press releases.
Material not cataloged by repository.
Research access not restricted. Photocopies provided.

RM 6/73

AMERICAN PALESTINE CAMPAIGN
2 boxes and 1 loose-leaf notebook, covering years 1931-1937.
In Zionist Archives and Library, New York City.
    Contains joint resolutions with the Keren Hayesod and the Jewish National Fund to centralize their organizations' programs because of common goals, and with the Joint Distribution Committee to aid European refugees by forming the UJA; minutes of the Executive, Administrative, and Emergency Committees (1932-1937); discussion of problems relating to cooperation between agencies and fund raising; financial reports concerning internal expenses and contributions and their disbursements; correspondence (among others, Louis Lipsky, 1931-1934); and fund-raising brochures.
Material not cataloged by repository.
Research access not restricted. Photocopies provided.

RM 6/73

AMERICAN RED MOGEN DAVID
1 folder, covering years 1948-1952.
In Zionist Archives and Library, New York City.
    Contains various pamphlets concerning the organization's activities in Israel and fund raising in America.
Material not cataloged by repository.
Research access not restricted. Photocopies provided.

RM 6/73

AMERICANS FOR HAGANAH
1 folder, covering years 1947-1948.
In Zionist Archives and Library, New York City.
Contains reports to the American people to gain moral and financial support for Israeli independence and a strong army.
Material not cataloged by repository.
Research access not restricted. Photocopies provided.

RM 6/73

AUSTER, DANIEL, 1893-1963
(b. Stanislav, Galicia; arrived in Eretz Yisrael in 1919; appointed deputy mayor of Jerusalem by High Commissioner, 1935; acting mayor, 1936-1938, 1944-1945; elected mayor, 1948-1951.)
1 item, dated 1948, in Record Group A297.
In Central Zionist Archives, Jerusalem.
Collection includes correspondence with Daniel Auster. Folder 40 contains correspondence on the Jewish Welfare Board of America support of the proposed Young Men's Hebrew Association in Jerusalem.
Collection cataloged by repository.
Research access not restricted. Photocopies available.

SG 10/81

BEHAM, ARIYEH, 1877-1941
(Director of the Pasteur Institute in Jerusalem; active in medical and public health activities in Palestine.)
5 items, covering years 1915-1916, interspersed in Record Group A60.
In Central Zionist Archives, Jerusalem.
Folder 31/b contains several items pertaining to American support of the Pasteur Institute in Palestine. Of special interest is a letter from Harry Friedenwald to Beham (March 9, 1915), promising publicity in America for the Pasteur Institute.
Material cataloged by repository.
Research access not restricted. Photocopies provided.

TzB 11/74

BEN-ZVI, YITZHAK, 1884-1963.
(2nd president of the State of Israel; born in Russia, emigrated to
Palestine in 1907; deported during World War I; went to the United
States where he reestablished Hechalutz together with David Ben-
Gurion in 1915; volunteered for the Jewish Legion in 1918 as a
means of returning to Palestine and was active in mobilization of
other volunteers.)
1 item, dated 1915, in private papers of Yitzhak Ben-Zvi (A116).
In Central Zionist Archives, Jerusalem.

Item is a letter in Hebrew, dated Tammuz, 5675 (Summer,
1915) from Avraham Shlomo of Jaffa, complaining that relief
supplies by American Jewry were demoralizing, that their distribution was causing friction and that living on relief tended to make
people stop working (Folder A 40/2).
Collection cataloged by repository.
Research access not restricted. Photocopies provided.

SS 7/74

BERKSON, ISAAC B., 1891-1975
(American educator; member of Palestine Executive of the Jewish
Agency 1931-1935).
Ca. 40 items, covering years 1930-1935, in Record Group A348.
In Central Zionist Archives, Jerusalem.

The collection includes letters, receipts, ledgers of contributions and reports concerning the following philanthropic projects;
work of Jessie Sampter with Yemenite children in Rehovoth and
the School for Deaf and Dumb Children in Tel Aviv (Folders 9
and 10), and distribution in Eretz Yisrael of Keren Ami Jewish
National Fund contributions collected in American Hebrew Schools
(Folders 9-12, 26 and 28).

Of special interest are the following items:

Letter from Jessie Sampter to Berkson, dated January 17,
1932 describing work at the School for Deaf and Dumb Children at
the Straus Health Center in Tel Aviv: "The responsibility for the
budget of $1,500 a year has been undertaken by a special committee
of the Palestine Lighthouse in New York, but until now the whole
budget has been raised through the efforts of Mrs. Stephen S. Wise"
(Folder 10).

Report of the Jewish Institute for the Blind, dated (in pencil) July, 1931, stating that contributions from the United States in 1930 accounted for two-thirds of the annual budget and that nine-tenths of the building fund was being held in the United States and the rest in Jerusalem (Folder 12).
Collection cataloged by repository.
Research access not restricted. Photocopies provided.

ML 11/81

BOARD OF DELEGATES OF AMERICAN ISRAELITES
(Established in 1859 by Rabbi Samuel Myer Isaacs as first national organization of Jewish congregations in the United States; it merged in 1878 with the Union of American Hebrew Congregations.)
1.   Ca. 100 items, covering years 1859-1878, interspersed in collection (I-2).
In American Jewish Historical Society, Waltham, Massachusetts.

The Board of Delegates was involved in several philanthropic ventures in Palestine. The collection contains the Proceedings of the Board of Delegates; references to activities in Palestine may be found in the Proceedings under the "Reports of the Executive Committee" during each of the following years: 1866; 1868; 1869 with Appendix A—Extract from Report of M. Netter to the Universal Israelite Alliance on Status of Jews in Palestine, and Appendix B—Correspondence on the subject of the Pilgrim Dwellings Near Jerusalem between Selig Hausdorff and Abraham Hart; 1870; 1871; 1872 with Appendix—Report on the Agricultural School at Jaffa. Occasional references to charitable donations to institutions in Palestine are contained in the minutes of the Board (1859-1870), the folder "Reports" (Box 3), an undated report on Palestine, the 1876 Executive Committee Report on Palestine, and the Treasurer's Report (including expenditures in Palestine) for the years 1871-1877.

References to philanthropic activities in Palestine are scattered throughout the correspondence of the Board:

Under the headings "Alliance Israélite Universelle," "Crémieux" and "Samuel, Sampson" there are letters concerning the Board of

Delegates' support of the Agricultural School at Jaffa during the years 1873-1875.

Under "Samuel, Sampson" and "Emanuel" there are reports of efforts on behalf of Palestine conducted with Moses Montefiore.

Under the headings "Montefiore," "Askenasi" and "Miscellaneous Folder" there is correspondence with the Haham Bashi chief rabbi of Jerusalem, Abraham Askenasi, concerning requests for funds.

The Board at times worked with the American Consulate in Jerusalem to aid indigent Jews who were American citizens. Such information is found under the headings "Lilienthal," and "Willson."

There is a file on Palestine (Box 4) that contains correspondence (1872-1873) between Selig Hausdorff and the Board of Delegates pertaining to contributions to the Bikur Holim Hospital and other charitable organizations in Jerusalem.

Collection cataloged by repository.
Research access not restricted. Photocopies provided.

MF 8/74

2.   1 item, dated 1877.
In American Jewish Archives, Cincinnati, Ohio.

Contained within the Proceedings and Correspondence of the Executive Committee is the following resolution adopted May, 1876:

1.   That the Board is opposed to the pauperization of our brethren in Palestine by means of indiscriminate charity which, it is currently believed, does not meet its objects, and will tend to the demoralization of the mass of the Jewish residents in the Holy Land.
2.   That the Board is of the opinion that aid should alone be given to the development of industrial pursuits, and the moral, social, and educational elevation of the people.
3.   That the Executive Committee be requested to communicate with the Board of Deputies of London, the Alliance Israélite Universelle, and the Berlin Committee for the Jerusalem Orphan Asylum, in order to agree upon a plan of joint action for the material elevation, and the moral and intellectual improvement of the Israelites of Palestine.

4.   That contributions for the benefit of the Jews of Palestine, and for the support of charitable institutions therein be suspended, and the amount appropriated for the Montefiore Memorial Fund be withheld until the Executive Committee shall render a report as to the best means of achieving the objects herein contemplated.

Material not cataloged by repository.
Research access not restricted. Photocopies provided.

RM 6/73

BRODIE, ISRAEL B., 1884-1965
(Born in Shavel, Lithuania; moved to Baltimore, Maryland in 1886; successful lawyer and businessman; cofounder of Palestine Economic Corporation and president of American Economic Committee.)
Ca. 50 items, covering years 1939-1947, interspersed and in special folders in Record Group A251.
In Central Zionist Archives, Jerusalem.
      The collection contains letters and reports of the American Palestine Fund (name changed to American Fund for Palestine Institutions, Inc. in July 1941) (Folders 3, 17a and 17b). Of interest is a proposal (April 8, 1939), to form an American Palestine Development Fund to allocate money to deserving and useful educational, cultural and social service institutions in Palestine, which would take the place of the more than 60 separate annual appeals being made at that time and not included in the newly organized United Jewish Appeal (Folder 17/a marked Edward A. Norman). Also of interest is a letter (March 11, 1947) to the UJA from Edward Norman, explaining why the American Fund will not combine their fund-raising efforts with the UJA (Folder 3).
Material cataloged by repository.
Research access not restricted. Photocopies provided.

OZ 1/75

CATHOLIC NEAR EAST RELIEF ASSOCIATION
(Catholic philanthropic association.)
2 folders, covering years 1922-1948 (M-141 and M-833).
In Archdiocese of Boston Archives, Brighton, Massachusetts.

Consists of correspondence and reports dealing with the work of the Association and archdiocesan contributions to its program. Collection not cataloged by repository.

Research access not restricted. Photocopies provided.

JDS 7/78

CENTRAL ZIONIST ARCHIVES, JERUSALEM, PHOTOGRAPH COLLECTION

(Photographs acquired by the CZA since its inception, arranged by accession number.)

7 items, covering years 192?-1945, interspersed in the collection. In Central Zionist Archives, Jerusalem.

A dictionary-catalog of names and subjects in Hebrew serves as index to the collection. Most of the items portray Nathan Straus (on a 1922 visit to Jerusalem, number 15,155) and the Health Center he donated (various years, in numbers 822-824, 6,457 and 13,191). Dorothy Thompson was photographed in the Hadassah Hospital, 1945, in front of a map of the United States showing origin of donations (number 5,912). A cornerstone-laying ceremony for a children's village in Ra'anana, sponsored by the Mizrachi Women's Organization of America, 1945, is in numbers 6,218-6,220. Collection cataloged by repository.

Research access not restricted. Copies (negative or positive) provided; permission necessary for further reproduction or publication.

YG 1/75

CENTRAL ZIONIST OFFICE, BERLIN

(Moved from Cologne to Berlin in 1911 because most members of the Inner Actions Committee elected at the 10th Zionist Congress resided there; absorbed the Commission for the Exploration of Palestine and the Palestine Department, which had led a separate existence in Berlin since 1903; transferred to London after the Annual Conference of 1920).

Ca. 700 items, covering years 1912-1918, interspersed and in special folders in Record Group Z3.

In Central Zionist Archives, Jerusalem.

The major part of the relevant material deals with the collection and expenditure of relief funds for the Jewish community of

Eretz Yisrael during World War I (Folders 60-61, 395, 757-760, 949, 1462 and 1471-1472). Of special interest are copies of a 6-page report in English, "Organizing Power of the American Relief Fund in Palestine," by H. H. Cohn (February, 1915), which claimed that "the educating power of the American Fund lies in its organizing power" (Folders 395 and 757). The arrival of relief supplies—food and medicine—aboard the U.S. ships *Des Moines* and *Vulcan* is the subject of correspondence in Folders 61, 758 and 1472. The distribution of American Relief Funds was the source of jealousies within the Jewish Community in Eretz Yisrael (Folders 759 and 1472). An attempt to dispatch an American medical unit in 1916 did not materialize, because permission was refused by the Turkish authorities (Folders 60 and 61).

Appeals for funds to Nathan Straus by Nahum Sokolow, the Federation of American Zionists and Dr. A. Ruppin for the Jewish community in Eretz Yisrael, both before and after the outbreak of World War I, are found in Folders 949 and 1471. Correspondence relating to donations for the Bezalel School and for the U.S. trip of its director, Prof. Boris Schatz, in 1912 can be found in Folders 754, 758-760 and 1448. Letters dealing with a proposed fund to build homes for Yemenite Jews in Eretz Yisrael (1912-1913) are located in Folders 756 and 947.

Collection cataloged by repository. (Record Group description available as mimeographed volume).

Research access not restricted. Photocopies provided.

OZ 6/75

CINCINNATI, OHIO, JEWISH NATIONAL FUND COUNCIL
2 folders, covering years 1935-1962, in Box 723.
In American Jewish Archives, Cincinnati, Ohio.

Contains minutes of the Council's meetings (11/35-2/38), records of donations to Haganah and fund-raising materials (letters, receipts and brochures).

Material not cataloged by repository.

Research access not restricted. Photocopies provided.

RM 6/73

COMMITTEE FOR A TEL AVIV YOUTH CENTER
1 item, undated.
In Zionist Archives and Library, New York City.

Item is a fund-raising pamphlet.
Material not cataloged by repository.
Research access not restricted. Photocopies provided.

RM 6/73

COUNCIL OF JEWISH FEDERATIONS AND WELFARE FUNDS
(An association of American communal organizations, established in
1932; among other activities, it reports on the programs and finan-
ces of national and overseas Jewish agencies.)
Ca. 150 items, covering years 1929-1948, in collection (I-69).
In American Jewish Historical Society, Waltham, Massachusetts.

The collection contains information on the fund-raising work,
budgets and activities, as well as miscellaneous correspondence
and some full audit reports of the American Fund for Palestinian
Institutions (1936-1948) (filed under American-Israel Cultural
Foundation); American Friends of the Hebrew University (1936-
1943); Avukah (1931-1944); Hadassah (1929-1948); the Jewish
National Fund (1930-1948); the Jewish Palestine Exploration
Society (1926-1931); and the United Palestine Appeal (1940-
1948), as well as some information on the Joint Distribution
Committee activities in Palestine (1934-1948). Also contains detailed
reports on the 1934 activities and budgets of some of the above as
well as the National Labor Committee for the Jewish Workers in
Palestine and the Mizrahi Palestine Fund (Box 190).

Of special interest is the 4-volume 1931 "Register of Jewish
Social Service Agencies in Palestine," updated and expanded by the
1938 volume "Palestine Yeshivoth and Charitable Agencies Currently
Appealing to Jewish Welfare Funds" (Box 188) and to 1935-1944
reports on overseas agencies receiving funds (Box 190), all of which
briefly describe the history, administration, activities, finances,
receipts and fund-raising methods of every Palestinian agency
appealing for funds in the United States. According to the 1931
compilation (Volume 1), U.S. citizens supplied 64 percent of the
budget needs of the 100 Palestinian institutions soliciting in the
United States during that year.
Collection cataloged by repository.
Research access not restricted. Photocopies provided.

JDS 6/75

DIAMOND, DAVID, 1898-1968
(Corporation counsel for the city of Buffalo; served 1 year as
N.Y. State Supreme Court Justice.)
Ca. 300 items and 1 loose-leaf notebook covering years 1941-1948,
interspersed in collection (P-59).
In American Jewish Historical Society, Waltham, Massachusetts.

Box 2 contains correspondence, speeches, membership lists,
minutes, etc. pertaining to the United Jewish Fund of Buffalo. Box 4
(in file "UJA Appeal") contains about 100 items of correspondence
concerning UJA appeals in Buffalo from 1941 to 1946.
Collection cataloged by repository.
Research access not restricted. Photocopies provided.

MF 10/74

ESCO FUND COMMITTEE, INC.
(Originally functioned through three separate foundations: ESCO
Fund Committee, Inc., organized in December, 1940; ESCO
Friends, Inc., organized in November, 1941; and ESCO Foundation
for Palestine, Inc., organized in 1942.)
63 boxes, covering 1941-1966.
In Columbia University, Library Special Collections, New York City.

The files contain correspondence, reports, newspaper clippings,
board minute books, photographs and ESCO publications relating to
the various projects undertaken by the three foundations. Among
the correspondents are Stephen S. Wise, Theodore Kollek, Ernest
Bloch and Leonard Bernstein.

The projects undertaken include a "Study of Economic and
Industrial Possibilities of the Development of Palestine" under the
direction of Dr. Emanuel Neumann of the AZEC, which was never
completed under ESCO's auspices due to an interorganizational
dispute, after which ECSO withdrew; a "Study of Arab-Jewish
Relations in Palestine with regard to social, economic and political
problems" (published by Yale University Press in 1946 under the
title *Palestine: Jewish, Arab, and British Policy*); a subvention to
Mailamm (American Palestine Music Association) in 1941 for record-
ing Babylonian and Yemenite traditional Jewish melodies, undertaken
in cooperation with the Department of Ethno-Musicology of Columbia
University; scholarships established in 1947 for Israeli composers to

come to Tanglewood to study; the purchase of a copy of the Arthur Szyk illustrated Haggadah for the Hebrew University Library in 1941; a grant to the Education Department of the Hebrew University in 1941 for a survey of vocational education in Palestine, the findings of which were used by the elementary school system in Palestine and Hadassah for planning future vocational training programs; a scholarship in occupational therapy in cooperation with Hadassah (1943); establishment of the ESCO Mechanical and Technical Department at the Pardes Hanna Agricultural Secondary School (1948), which eventually funded the Stephen S. Wise Room on Comparative Religion at the Hebrew University National Library; and the establishment of a loan fund for American students at the Hebrew University (1946).

Collection cataloged by repository.

Research access restricted. Photocopies provided.

RM 1/73

FRANKFURTER, FELIX, 1882-1965

(U.S. Supreme Court Justice 1939-1962; associated with the Brandeis group in American Zionism; member of the delegation to the Paris Peace Conference in 1919; withdrew from formal participation in the Zionist Organization of America after 1921 but maintained an active interest in Zionist affairs.)

13 items, covering years 1915, 1918, 1931-1932 and 1939-1940, interspersed in the private papers of Felix Frankfurter (A264).

In Central Zionist Archives, Jerusalem.

Collection contains correspondence and documents pertaining to American Jewish involvement in providing relief for the Jewish community in Palestine during World War I (Folder 1), the Hebrew University (Folders 20, 26, 43 and 45) and a request by Judah L. Magnes to aid Palestinian artists in 1940 to become better acquainted with Dutch art (Folder 49).

Collection cataloged by repository.

Research access not restricted. Photocopies provided.

TzB 10/74

FRIEDENWALD, HARRY, 1864-1950.

(Medical doctor; longtime active Zionist; president and honorary

president of the Federation of American Zionists, 1904-1918; acting chairman of the Zionist Commission in Palestine, 1919; visited Palestine on various occasions.)
Ca. 65 items, covering years 1920-1947, interspersed and in special folders in Record Group A182.
In Central Zionist Archives, Jerusalem.

American interest in and philanthropy to schools appears in Folders 4 and 48; to Hadassah in Folders 31 and 55; and to the JDC in Folder 31 (Folder 32 also contains correspondence about the American Zionist Medical Unit and Shaare Zedek hospital). Correspondence about the Palestine Jewish Medical Association is found in Folder 54 and Shaare Zedek hospital is also mentioned in Folder 50.

Of special interest is a 5-page letter from the director of the American Zionist Medical Unit to Louis Lipsky (January 1, 1922) in which is mentioned the problem of retaining the American character of the unit (Folder 46).
Material cataloged by repository.
Research access not restricted. Photocopies provided.

TzB 1/75

GERMAN CONSULATES IN PALESTINE
8 items, dated 1924-1928 and 1932, in Record Group 67.
In Israel State Archives, Jerusalem.

Folder 1378 contains a speech by Judah L. Magnes and correspondence with the German consul regarding American fund raising on behalf of the Hebrew University, noting contributions by the American Jewish Physicians' Committee; $100,000 for the Humanities Building; funds provided by the Joint Distribution Committee, American Friends of the Hebrew University and Mrs. Felix Warburg; the American Academic Assistance Committee for placement of dismissed German scholars at the Hebrew University and the expressed fear that German influence at the university was endangered by the activities of Judah Magnes and by the substantial American financial support of the institution.

Of special interest is a copy of a 2-page memo dated April 5, 1924 from German consul Karl Kapp to the Foreign Office in Berlin regarding the establishment and organization of the Institute of

Chemistry at the Hebrew University, whose microbiology section was organized by the American Jewish Physicians' Committee after Albert Einstein's visit to America in Spring, 1921.
Collection cataloged by repository.
Research access not restricted. Photocopies provided.

TG/ML 1/82

GRATZ FAMILY
(Prominent colonial Jewish family in Philadelphia; Barnard Gratz, a native of Poland, emigrated from London to Pennsylvania in 1754.)
2 items, dated 1753, in collection (P-8).
In American Jewish Historical Society, Waltham, Massachusetts.
    The items are two Hebrew letters from Palestine requesting financial assistance.
Collection cataloged by repository.
Research access not restricted. Photocopies provided.

MF 9/74

GREAT BRITAIN, CONSULATE IN JERUSALEM
2 items, dated 1853, in File 9 in Record Group 123/1.
In Israel State Archives, Jerusalem.
    The items consist of handwritten copies of two letters notarized by the mayor of Philadelphia, Pennsylvania and dated March 30, 1853 with the seal of the U.S. Consulate in Beirut. The first letter, from editors M. Engles and John Leyborn of the weekly religious journal *The Presbyterian*, published in Philadelphia, protests the misuse by John Meshullam of funds collected via their journal for the agricultural project at Artas, described to them by Clorinda Minor. In the second letter, Mr. J. L. Boyd of the Agricultural and Manual Labour School of Palestine responds that the money received by his agency was delivered only to the school.
Collection cataloged by repository.
Research access not restricted. Photocopies provided.

TG 4/81

HADASSAH, THE WOMEN'S ZIONIST ORGANIZATION OF AMERICA

(Largest Zionist organization in the world; established in 1912; conducts programs both in Israel and the United States.)

1.   Relevant material found in several hundred file-cabinet drawers, covering years 1912-1948, located in Central Files and Records Division.

In Hadassah, New York City.

Included are the Hadassah Central Committee minutes (January 5, 1921-November 8, 1921) (bound in Hadassah National Board Minutes, Set 2, Book 1, with June 15, 1921 in National Executive Committee Minutes, Set 1, Book 1); National Executive Board minutes (December 5, 1921-September 23, 1925; July 10, 1929-1948) (bound in National Executive Board Minutes, Set 1, Books 1-12); and Executive Committee minutes (October 2, 1924-1948) (bound in Executive Committee Minutes, Set 1, Books 1-4, with January 22, 1947-1948) (bound in National Board Minutes and Executive Committee Minutes, Set 2, Books 11-12), whose discussions concern the Nurses' Training School and scholarships for American women to study there; the Red Mogen David (concerning cooperation and coordination of efforts to avoid duplication); the Orphans' Fund; Restoration Fund; work of local chapters (e.g., adoption of Palestinian Jewish orphans) and Junior Hadassah Units; the Hadassah Palestine Circle and the Hadassah Palestine Supplies Department of America (e.g., supplying mosquito nets, clothing for Ezrat Nashim in Jerusalem, wool for clothing orphans, etc.); the Chicago Palestine Welfare Committee (concerning contributions to the Nurses' Training School); Mrs. Chaim Weizmann's appeal to aid in fund raising for the Women's International Zionist Organization through its Jewel Fund; publications (concerning establishing new chapters throughout the United States and increasing membership of existing chapters); Hadassah's relationship with Keren Hayesod, the American Jewish Congress, the Joint Distribution Committee, the Zionist Organization of America, the National Council of Jewish Women, the JNF, United Palestine Appeal, etc.; financial support of the Rutenberg Project; infant welfare work; work of the Hadassah office in Palestine and of internal affairs in the United States' Hadassah Building Fund; cooperation with the

American Jewish Physicians' Committee regarding plans to open a medical school and University Hospital at the Hebrew University; Hadassah Medical Relief Association; participation in the Schweitzer Hospital in Tiberias, the Haifa Hospital, the Rothschild Hospital and the Safed Hospital; various financial matters (both internal U.S. and funding for Israel operations); the Meier Schfeyah Orphanage (funding by Junior Hadassah); midwife services; Penny Luncheon Fund (for school lunches); reports and letters from Henrietta Szold, Irma Lindheim, Rose Halprin and others concerning Hadassah's operations and progress of the *Yishuv*; Palestine Committee Reports; free medical service for Jewish police in Palestine; playgrounds; clothing distribution; rescue work (begun as a protest against Nazi persecutions in 1933), including Youth Aliyah, especially placement of children from Europe and the Middle East, and refugee transport to Palestine; Arab disturbances and the role of Hadassah facilities in treating the injured; immigration restrictions (the 1939 White Paper) and their significance for the *Yishuv* and Hadassah's work; Dr. Mordecai M. Kaplan's address to Hadassah asking that they be an instrument for creating Jewish consciousness; Szold and Brandeis forests; Zionist educational programs; school hygiene programs; Hadassah pilgrimages; support for the Palestine Pavilion at the 1939 New York World's Fair; financial support for children's education projects in Palestine, including discussions of different ideas behind educational programs proposed and implemented; financial support for Kfar Szold; Zionist education projects in the United States, including camps; vocational training programs, including involvement with the Deborah Kallen School; planting of memorial forests and gardens; post-World War II refugee problems; fund-raising activities; question of membership in and continued support of the American Jewish Conference; opposition to continuance of White Paper policy after World War II and the urging of President Harry S Truman to support immigration of refugees into Palestine; immigrant health care in Palestine; the 1946 Anglo-American Committee of Inquiry; political maneuverings in the United States for U.S. Government support and work toward establishing the Jewish State; reports delivered by delegates upon their return from World Zionist congresses; immigrant medical aid, including establishment of field hospitals; post-World War II *Aliyah* from America, replacing lost potential *Chalutzim* from Europe; mental health programs in

Palestine for survivors of concentration camps; combatting growing pro-Revisionist sentiment in the United States; American interns at the Hadassah-Hebrew University Hospital; problem of partition concerning Hadassah's facilities in Jerusalem; the Mt. Scopus massacre; growing tensions with Arabs; and Hadassah's mobilization to aid the newly emerging State of Israel.

Also bound are Financial Reports (October, 1936-September 30, 1947); Annual Convention Proceedings (1914 [photocopy, original at Central Zionist Archives], 1930, 1932, 1937-1938 and 1944-1948) and Mid-Winter Convention Proceedings for 1947. In addition, 4 file drawers contain minutes or transcripts of Convention Proceedings, (1914-1948) financial and activity reports, addresses delivered, lists of delegates, resolutions passed, round-table agendas, National Board Meeting minutes, constitutional amendments, entertainment (plays, films), etc., with some duplication of material found in the officially bound Convention Proceedings mentioned above.

Found in the collection is a bound volume of the "Abridged notes of Rear Admiral Charles S. Stephenson (MC) USN (Retired). Log File on Inspection Trip in Palestine (August 3-September 15, 1944—urban and rural areas)," a 345-page detailed account, including numerous photographs, of Jewish and Arab health problems (malaria, typhoid, tuberculosis, rickets, venereal diseases, malnutrition, trachoma, etc.), health programs (including mental health care, prenatal care, child welfare and health inspections, school hygiene, dental clinics, nutrition and nutrition education, health education, day nursery and kindergarten at Hadassah's facilities, and preventive medicine), health facilities, medical personnel, bio-medical research, working conditions, sanitation facilities, slaughtering houses, living conditions in immigrant camps, medical education with recommendations for improving health conditions and operations, school meal programs and home visits; it also describes the tendency for Jews to blame the Arabs for the disease-carrying flies, and vice versa, when both appear responsible, and characterizes Ben-Gurion as potentially "ruthless if he had complete authority," a man "more interested in politics than he is in the health of his people."

Also found is a 7-volume "Henrietta Szold and Youth Aliyah Manuscript based on a collection of Henrietta Szold's letters for the period 1934-1944, by Zena Harman," volume 1 being an account of H. Szold's work, Hadassah's involvement (financial, as well as through gifts of clothing and other material), a history of Youth Aliyah (including a 5-page memorandum by Emma Ehrlich as spokesperson for Youth Aliyah, correcting the Harman manuscript from its recollection and perspective), with subsequent volumes being correspondence and reports (originals in the archives of Jewish Agency, Department for Child and Youth Immigration). (A second copy is found in the Permanent Files section following folder marked "Affidavits 1940.")

Periodicals include *Hadassah Headlines* (name originally *Hadassah Chapter Instructions*) (1933-1948, most issues); a news bulletin of projects and workings of Hadassah; and *The Hadassah Newsletter* (1914-1948) (later *Hadassah Magazine*, originally *Hadassah Bulletin*).

The following material is located in file cabinets and described under the labeled designations found on the drawer:

HISTORY

Chapters & Regions and Biographies—correspondence, reports, and memos regarding history of local Hadassah chapters and prominent members.

YOUTH ALIYAH

In a series of folders (1938-1946) found in 7-file cabinet drawers are circular letters, statistical reports, pamphlets, press releases, clippings, correspondence (particularly from H. Szold and Hans Beyth), cables, etc., regarding operations of Youth Aliyah; Refugee Economic Corporation funding of Youth Aliyah and other financial matters concerning Youth Aliyah; Jewish Agency involvement in Youth Aliyah; case histories of Youth Aliyah members; fund-raising activities and meetings (at homes of Mrs. Lehman and Fannie Hurst, at the Harmonie Club, etc.); copies of H. Szold's letters to supporting organizations in the United States, Palestine, etc., concerning Youth Aliyah operations, and to children in Palestine seeking to give them encouragement (copies of letters in Harman volumes noted above); letters from European offices of Youth Aliyah, many appealing to the Palestine office and to H. Szold in particular to speed up operations; the *Struma* and *Patria* affairs; Kfar Szold; H. Szold's visits to Youth Aliyah camps; and Bernard

Gelbart's report on Youth Aliyah (original manuscript with drawings). These files are found in a rear corner. In a second location, the center aisle, is a drawer marked Youth Aliyah, which contains a folder marked "*Dushkin, Alexander #1*", which includes "Educational Achievements and Problems of Youth Aliyah in Eretz Yisrael: Report Submitted to Hadassah", October, 1947.

MEDICAL

Adler, Saul—correspondence and clippings regarding Hadassah Medical Organization's (HMO) funding of Dr. Adler's trip from Palestine to International Congress of Tropical Medicine & Malaria in Washington.

Blood Bank (HMO RHUH)—12 folders regarding the operations of the HMO Rothschild-Hebrew University Hospital Blood Bank, 1946-1948.

Cancer-Max Schloessinger Fund—correspondence concerning the early operations of the Fund in Palestine, including cases aided, 1944-1946.

Cohen, Ethel April—correspondence concerning her application to participate in the establishment of social service department of the Hadassah Medical School.

Committees—Hadassah Medical Organization, December, 1947-June, 1948—minutes (December 1, 1947-June 22, 1948) concerning its operations in Palestine (medical) and the United States (administrative and fund-raising), and other internal affairs.

Cyprus—correspondence, reports, and clippings concerning conditions in Cyprus camps and Hadassah's attempts to alleviate them, 1946-1948.

Electroencephelographic Unit—correspondence and clippings concerning the purchase and maintenance of an EEG machine for the new neurological department of Hadassah Hospital with the aid of donations from the Boston chapter, 1947-1948.

Fellowships—Budget and Finances #1—"Summary of Scholarships Granted Under HMO Medical Fellowship Funds" as of January 1, 1948; includes also a listing of researchers, areas of research and amounts granted.

Fellowship—Kliger, I. J., Dr.—file of a fellowship recipient.

Hadassah Council in Palestine—minutes of meeting of the Hadassah Council in Palestine (June 3, 1947), "Report of the Institutions of Hadassah . . . " submitted to the 22nd Zionist Congress (December, 1946), and correspondence concerning Palestine operations.

Hadassah Medical Organization #1–"Five Year Program for the HMO," submitted by Yassky.

Hebrew University Hadassah Medical School #1–correspondence and reports on the establishment and organization of the Medical School, 1946-1947.

Hebrew University Hadassah Medical School–Budget and Finance–Building Fund Campaign #1–"Minutes of Meetings of Executive Committee of American Friends of the Hebrew University & Hebrew University–Hadassah Medical School Campaign" (April 24, 1947; August 20, 1947; November 18, 1947; January 20, 1948; February 3, 1948; February 19, 1948); correspondence and clippings concerning raising funds for establishment of the Medical School.

Hebrew University Hadassah Medical School–Departments–Dentistry, School of, #1–correspondence (1946-1948), reports and "Memo on Meeting with Representatives of the Alpha Omega Fraternity" (February 11, 1945), concerning establishment of a dental school at the Hebrew University.

Hebrew University Hadassah Medical School–History–two reports by Charles S. Stephenson, "Comparative Notes of Health Conditions in Palestine" (1944) and "Survey of Health and Hospital Conditions in Palestine" (abridged) (1946): The next 3 folders, variously marked "Medical School Campaign and History," contain materials (correspondence, reports, charts, public relations used, etc.) concerning establishment of the Medical School.

Hebrew University–Jerusalem–Affiliation Agreements #1–affiliation agreements for 1936, 1940-1942 and 1945; correspondence concerning them.

Histories–several brief histories of Hadassah's activities in Palestine, and also a copy of the *Hadassah Bulletin* published in Jerusalem August 11, 1922.

Infant Welfare–an extensive report (1923), "Infant Welfare and Milk Distribution Work in Palestine," and several lesser reports (1922-1927); also two circular letters and a money collection pouch (1922) for the Palestine Milk Station Fund.

Ophthalmology–Trachoma–translations of a lecture by Dr. N. Dobrzynski given at the Jubilee Conference of the Jewish Physicians' Association, Jerusalem, September, 1944 ("The Anti-Trachoma Campaign in Palestine in the Past and the Present") and of "Proposals submitted in connection with the convention of Ophthalmologists active in Anti-Trachoma Campaign" (compiled by Dr. T. Rosental).

Palestine School Luncheons–(folder labeled "HMO School Luncheon Fund 1932-1934" but filed under PSL)–material dating from 1925-1935, among which are the minutes of meetings of the Penny School Luncheon Fund (June 15, 1926, November 30, 1926), statistical reports of meals served (August, 1925-September, 1926), correspondence (much of it from Sophia Berger of the Palestine Orphan Committee of the JDC and from Henrietta Szold) concerning present operations (including financial data) and problems arising at the several schools that were being serviced and future plans; also circulars, pamphlets and a "Shalach Mones" collection envelope.

Postgraduate Institute–"Tentative Programme of a Post-Graduate Course for Prospective Medical Officers of the State of Israel, Under the Auspices of the Hebrew University and Hadassah Medical Organization" (May 17, 1948).

Rothschild Hadassah University Hospital (RHUH)–Henrietta Szold's letter of 1922 to Baron Edmond de Rothschild, thanking him for hearing her plea for aid for health work, and her "Memorandum on the Rothschild Hospital with Reference to the Damiani Property," discussing the cooperation between Hadassah and the American Jewish Physicians' Committee to establish a hospital as necessary for the fulfillment of their health plans (1926).

Schweitzer, Peter J., Memorial Hospital–"Excerpts from the Report on the Activities of the Schweitzer Hospital in Tiberias during 1939-1940," "Activities of the Schweitzer Hospital Tiberias 1940 and 1941," and a letter to Schweitzer thanking him for his continued financial assistance to the hospital.

Simon, Herman, Memorial Fund–correspondence (1936-1938) between Hadassah and the Simon Memorial Fund concerning their $2,500 contribution to the RHUH.

Singer, Edward, Dr.–correspondence (1948) concerning *Aliyah* to aid the emerging state.

Straus, Nathan and Lina, Health Center–bound Annual Reports (1932-1935, 1937-1938).

Straus, Nathan, Health Center Dedication–copy of a letter from Lina Straus to H. Szold acknowledging the Strauses' intention to erect the Health Center; also a program of the Cornerstone Ceremonies (March 2, 1927), and the *Hadassah News Letter* of May, 1929, discussing the dedication ceremonies.

Straus, Nathan & Lina, Health Center Endowment Fund– material (1926-1938), including minutes of a meeting of the representatives of the Committee of the Health Centers in Jerusalem and Tel Aviv (March 2, 1928); Straus' power of attorney to J. L. Magnes, H. Szold, et al. (December 21, 1926); memos; correspondence; financial records of donations, etc.; and clippings concerning the funding and appropriating of the fund.

Straus, Nathan & Lina, Health Center Hygiene Museum– correspondence (1928-1930) concerning establishment and funding of a Hygiene Museum in Jerusalem and Tel Aviv, including a $6,500 contribution to the Jerusalem museum from the Chicago Palestine Welfare Committee.

Tel Aviv Municipal Hospital–1939 correspondence between I. Rokach, mayor of Tel Aviv, and H. Yassky, and between Yassky and H. Szold concerning the deterioration of health facilities in Tel Aviv after their being turned over to the municipality, with a brief discussion of the possibility of Hadassah's resuming its management of the hospital.

Tuberculosis–1945-1946 program plans ("A Rehabilitation Program for the Tuberculous," construction plans for the Hadassah T. B. Hospital in Jerusalem, by Yassky), architects' plans for the hospital, and excerpts of minutes of meetings of several committees concerning the hospital (January, 1946-June, 1946).

Yassky, Haim, Clinic–Yassky's covering letter and memo (1943) concerning "Problems for Consideration with HMO's Tasks During the Period of Reconstruction" at the conclusion of World War II.

Yassky, Haim, Dr., Estate–report delivered by Yassky at Park Central Hotel (January 21, 1945) concerning health conditions in Palestine, Yassky's thoughts on Hadassah's future role in Palestine at the Hadassah National Board Meeting (February 14, 1945), a Five-Year Plan by Yassky (1945), and a biography following his murder.

GENERAL FILES

Brandeis, Louis D.—two undated addresses and typescripts of letters to numerous Zionist leaders (1930-1941) with suggestions for future Zionist work (e.g., gaining more volunteer work from members).

Child Welfare Circulated Letters 1938-1940—circular letters and "Chapter Instructions" clippings for fund raising for child welfare programs in Palestine.

Eban, Abba—typescript of an address delivered by Maj. Aubrey Eban to the Executive Board of Hadassah (May 23, 1947) on the political future of the *Yishuv* and Jewish-Arab relations.

Financial Loans, 1946-1948—correspondence, cables, and reports concerning loans made by Hadassah from Palestine banks.

Financial Welfare Funds—financial reports of Youth Aliyah, December, 1944 and October, 1945.

Goldmann, Nahum—typescript of an address delivered by Dr. Goldmann to the National Board of Hadassah October 28, 1946, concerning Palestine political developments in mid-1946.

Hadassah Chronology—several chronological accounts of Hadassah history (from 1912).

HMRA Certificate of Incorporation—photocopy of certificate of incorporation of Hadassah Medical Relief Association, Inc. (December, 1940), whose stated purpose is to "provide medical relief for and minister to the physical well-being of needy persons in Palestine; to support and maintain public hospitals, medical service in immigrant camps, schools, agricultural settlements, infant welfare stations, and clinics to relieve sickness and distress and to prevent plagues and diseases in Palestine. In connection therewith it shall be within the purpose of such corporation to use as means to the above purposes, research, publication and establishment and maintenance of charitable and public activities, agencies and institutions, and the aid of any such agencies and institutions already established, including nurses' training schools, all of which purposes shall be carried out solely in the territory of Palestine."

Halprin, Mrs. Samuel (Rose)—several folders of correspondence (1931-1934, 1941-1944) concerning activities of Hadassah in

Palestine and Palestine political matters (e.g., 1939 White Paper); also concerning internal affairs of Hadassah and personal affairs of Mrs. Halprin.

Herzog, Rabbi Isaac and Mrs.—correspondence and excerpts of minutes concerning Herzog Fund, a $10,000 grant from Hadassah originally for the emigration of young rabbis in China and Europe (1947) but reallocated for research and housing improvements among the Orthodox groups in Palestine.

Jacobs, E., Memorial—address by Mrs. Edward Jacobs (January 7, 1941) presented to the National Board of Hadassah, entitled "Review of Hadassah's Role in Political Zionism."

Jacobs, Rose and Edward—statement of Mrs. Rose Jacobs presented to the representative of Hadassah and the Women's International Zionist Organization concerning women's role in the *Yishuv*, contained in a letter (June 3, 1930) to Col. F. H. Kisch of the Jewish Agency; also a memo (December 1, 1936) concerning strengthening of the national organization of Hadassah in the United States.

Junior Hadassah Constitution—copy of 1941 amended Constitution, whose stated purpose was to: "promote the establishment of a legally assured, publicly secured home for the Jewish people in Palestine. To carry on Palestinian work, (a) primarily such as relates to child-care and education; (b) the health work, which is the program of Senior Hadassah; (c) all other undertakings included in the Zionist Platform. To foster Zionist ideals and education in America. To carry on JNF work. To cooperate with other existing Zionist groups."

Junior Hadassah—printed material concerning Meier Schfeyah Children's Village; H. Szold School of Nursing; 1921, 1923 and 1925 anniversary programs of Junior Hadassah.

History of Junior Hadassah—copy of a paper on history of Junior Hadassah.

"Forty Years of Junior Hadassah"—a large envelope in front of this folder, containing a history of Meier Schfeyah Village (30 years of Hadassah involvement), a 1921 circular letter concerning graduation of first nursing class from Alice Seligsberg, resolutions of Junior Hadassah Convention in Pittsburgh (June, 1924), A. Seligsberg's history of the early days of Hadassah (1912-1916), circular letters (H. Szold's "Familiar Letter from Palestine No. 6," February 1, 1922; Sophia Berger, 1927; etc.), correspondence (Louis D. Brandeis, H. Szold, Sophia Berger and C. N. Bialik), concerning Youth Aliyah and other activities, and clippings—much of which material deals more with Hadassah than with Junior Hadassah.

Kaplan, Dr. Mordecai M.—transcript of an address by Kaplan (1950) in which he recounts his early association (beginning 1904) with H. Szold and several meetings at his home of the group that later assumed the name Hadassah, including the meeting at which the American Zionist Medical Unit was first discussed.

Lindheim, Irma—circular letter addressed to the National Board of Hadassah (July 26, 1943) in which she put forth her analysis of and recommendations for improving Zionist Youth Work in America.

Louison, Evelyn, Fund—correspondence (1928-1935) and legal papers for the trust fund established by the Portland Chapter of Hadassah to endow a bed in the Rothschild Hospital.

Mack, Julian (Judge)—obituary clippings and memo discussing plans for memorial services to be held by Hadassah.

Medical Advisory Board—minutes, March, 1943-April, 1946.

Roosevelt, Franklin D.—material including 1938 Hadassah Convention open letter to Roosevelt seeking his support for establishment of a Jewish State, letters of best wishes to Hadassah conventions (1938, 1939 and 1944), etc.

Rosensohn, Samuel J., Memorial Fund—memos and correspondence (1939-1947) concerning memorial fund establishing "Shelf" at Hebrew University Library.

Seligsberg, Alice—several brief biographies.

PALESTINE PARTITION & ARAB-JEWISH RELATIONS COM—MITTEE 1942-1943

Contains "Hadassah Committee for the Study of Arab-Jewish Relations Material" prepared by Moshe Perlmann; various pamphlets from American Jewish Committee, American Jewish Conference and other sources concerning Arab-Jewish relations and the Partition Question; excerpt from minutes of Palestine Council of Hadassah (January 19, 1941) and from minutes of the Guggenheimer-Hadassah Recreation Committee (April 23, 1941) concerning mixed playgrounds; "Memorandum on Jerusalem Under Partition Submitted to the Palestine Partition Commission by the Jewish Agency for Palestine" (1938); and "Memorandum to the Palestine Partition Commission submitted by Mr. Ussischkin." Also found here is a "Memorandum Submitted to the Palestine Royal Commission by Hadassah, The Women's Zionist Organization of America, on American Jewish Interest in Medical and Health Welfare Work in Palestine" (1937).

NATIONAL BOARD PERSONNEL–PALESTINE ECONOMIC CORPORATION

This file drawer contains the personal files of the National Board members (mostly correspondence and memos, 1944-1946) concerning internal affairs of Hadassah and specific activities of the board members. Of importance is the "Report of Jewish Agency Executive Meeting in Paris by Mrs. Moses P. Epstein at Regular Summer Executive Meeting of Hadassah" (August 21, 1946) (in Mrs. M. Epstein II folder); "Statement of Mrs. Judith Epstein, Representing Hadassah, the Women's Zionist Organization of America to the Anglo-American Committee of Inquiry" (January 8, 1946); articles and addresses of Tamar de Sola Pool on Palestine in post-World War II, etc.; and a letter from a Rabbi Julian F. Feingold of Adath Israel Temple of Cleveland, Mississippi (December 12, 1945), which states, "I would welcome most earnestly an attempt of Hadassah to organize in Cleveland. Let me explain the difficulties that we must expect to encounter. The former Rabbi in Cleveland, while not a member of the American Council for Judaism, nevertheless leaned in their direction, and to the best of my knowledge no Rabbi has preached Zionism from the pulpit here. Last year I preached so many Zionist sermons that I am afraid I was regarded as somewhat of a missionary. This year about four sermons have been devoted to Palestine. The Jewish flag flies now in our Temple, and yet withstanding all there is a definite anti-Zionist sentiment which could break out even to the extent of dividing the community. This group is for the most part uninformed and yet they are intoxicated by so-called American religious security. Any attempt at Hadassah in Cleveland must reach this group in order to succeed"; "Proposal Regarding the Principles of Reorganization of Public Health and Social Welfare Activities in the Poorer Quarters of Jerusalem (Tourover #2).

VERY OLD BEQUESTS—LOUIS D. BRANDEIS

This file drawer contains records from the 1920s of bequests from individuals and organizations for the RHUH, Nurses' Textbook Fund, Baby Fund, Diabetes Fund, land purchase for Hadassah, etc.; also contains the files of Brandeis, including general correspondence (1920-1941) offering advice on problems facing Hadassah, articles by and about him, material concerning his bequest to Hadassah, memorials and tributes following his death, etc.

1944-1946—HENRIETTA SZOLD—U.S. DEPARTMENTS

H. Szold Foundation—four folders of correspondence, memos, excerpted minutes, etc. concerning the H. Szold Foundation Fund used for scholarships, child welfare work, HMO, etc.

1944-1946—PA-SHULMAN

Palestine Committee—four folders containing the minutes of the Palestine Committee 1944-1946, and an extensive index of their contents detailing the discussion regarding Hadassah's activities in Palestine.

Palestine Supplies—circular letters and pamphlets appealing for new and used supplies for Palestine, and monthly accountings of donations.

HADASSAH MEDICAL ORGANIZATION

(For more material concerning 1918-1944, cf. file cabinet in corner; for more concerning 1946-1948, cf. drawer in center aisle near Permanent Files labeled "World's Fair Material" and at front of drawer marked "Permanent Files—J. L. Magnes.") The following represents a large collection of material found in some 23 file drawers (in 2 locations) (1918-1948). The vast majority of this material, consisting of correspondence, reports, memos, excerpted minutes, clippings, etc., centers around the following areas: American Zionist Medical Unit; Dr. H. Yassky's Weekly Letters (periodic reports of HMO activities); RHUH, Haifa, Tel Aviv, and Tiberias Hospitals; Straus Health Center; budget and finances (including statistical reports); nurses' training; Hebrew University (groundbreaking and building plans); Kupat Holim; confidential report by HMO in Palestine concerning establishment of relations with Palestine Zionist Executive (including correspondence and other related material); report of the Jewish National Assembly (1930-1932); infant welfare; immigrants; donations; school luncheon program;

Guggenheimer Recreation Project; preventive health work—malaria control; youth services; medical school; playground; Mogen David Adom; Lemaan Hayeled; TB and X-ray therapy; Vaad Leumi; and nutrition.

PERMANENT FILES: "Agreements and Contracts"

Affidavits 1940—correspondence, cables, memos, and affidavits from, to or concerning refugees from German-occupied Europe, concerning chances of their emigration to the United States or Palestine.

Agreements and Contracts—Allied Jewish Appeal—March 7, 1930 agreement between the JDC, the American section of the Administrative Committee of Jewish Agency, Keren Hayesod, Hod, and the Mizrachi Organization of America "to unite the forces of American Jewry in order that the funds required for the activities of the JDC and the Jewish Agency for Palestine may be obtained with the utmost success and economy."

Agreements and Contracts—American Jewish Physicians' Committee—series of agreements and correspondence concerning them (1923-1937), between Hadassah and the AJPC concerning establishment of and maintenance of Hadassah Hospital, the Nursing School and Medical School.

Agreements and Contracts—Misc.—in order as found, the following agreements: "Agreement on principles between Hadassah and the American Friends of the Hebrew University to conduct a joint drive for the establishment of an undergraduate medical school by Hebrew University and Hadassah" (1947); "Draft Agreement to be Used as Basis for Negotiations with Zionist Authorities on the subject of Future Relations to the HMO in Palestine" (n.d.); "Trust Deed" (July 29, 1941) establishing the H. Szold Fund, including its operational specifications; two affidavits by Samuel J. Rosensohn as secretary (May 29, 1923 and August 22, 1923) detailing establishment, work of and purposes of the Palestine Development Council; agreements between Hadassah and the UPA concerning Hadassah's participation in the UPA for the year October, 1926-October, 1927 (November, 1926) and for Hadassah's fund raising and promotion of Youth Aliyah (December 9, 1935); draft agreement between ZOA, Hadassah, JDC and Keren Hayesod for "administration of the work of the HMO in Palestine, of hospitals, nurses' training schools and polyclinics . . . to be vested in a Governing Board consisting of six members, two to be appointed by the JDC, and the remaining two to be named by the four thus appointed" (May 1, 1923); confirmation of the above draft, to begin May 1, 1924; and an agreement between the House of Rothschild in Paris through its Palestine representatives, the PICA and the Joint Committee of Hadassah and the American Jewish Physicians' Committee to permit them "to occupy the house in Jerusalem known as the Meyer de Rothschild Hospital for 20 years from this date on condition that the whole complex be used only for hospital purposes" (June 3, 1926).

Agreements and Contracts—Jewish National Fund—1926 agreement between Hadassah and JNF to promote the latter's work (includes also record of monies collected April 15, 1926-April 30, 1927, minutes of first meeting of the JNF Council of Hadassah March 1, 1926 and "Program of Work of the JNF Council of Hadassah") and January 4, 1933 agreement deeding Hadassah land to JNF to build an expansion onto the Central Hadassah Hospital in Jerusalem.

Agreements and Contracts—Youth Aliyah—1935 agreement and related correspondence (1935-1945) concerning Hadassah's pledge to work for (fund raising) and support (e.g., through promotion) Youth Aliyah.

Agreements and Contracts—Medical School—"Agreement of Affiliation and Relationship Between the Hebrew University and Hadassah, the Women's Zionist Organization of America for the Purposes of Graduate Medical Teaching and Research" (July 31, 1934); also the "Master Plan—Development of Medical Center and School" (February 18, 1946) and a historical "Chronology of Medical School Plans" (June, 1946).

Agreements and Contracts—Straus Health Center—September 15, 1921 agreement to deed Nathan Straus Health Bureau to Hadassah (retaining the name of its donor); December 21, 1926 agreement to donate $250,000 "for establishment and maintenance of such charitable institution in Jerusalem, to be known as the Nathan and Lina Straus Health Center"; and July 12, 1928 agreement to donate $75,000 for a similar facility, under the same name, in Tel Aviv; also related correspondence.

Agreements and Contracts—World Zionist Organization—April 6, 1927 agreement specifying relations between Hadassah and the World Zionist Organization.

Agreements and Contracts—ZOA—agreements and related correspondence (1923-1925 and 1933) concerning relations between ZOA and Hadassah defining respective provinces.

Change of Name—legal papers concerning 1925 and 1947 Hadassah name changes; also a chronological listing of names of the organization—1912, Hadassah Chapter of Daughters of Zion; between 1912 and 1916, Federation of Women Zionist Societies; 1916, Hadassah; 1922, Hadassah, Inc.; 1925, Hadassah, the Women's Zionist Organization of America, Inc. (cf. also Certificate of Incorporation folder).

Certificate of Incorporation—1922 certificate of incorporation.

Certificate of Increases in the Number of Directors—certificates for 1925 and 1935.

(In drawer marked "Confidential A-Z")

History—Children to Palestine—circular materials (1944-1948) from this organization, a "national committee initiated and led by Christians who believe that the rescue and establishment of Jewish orphans overseas should not be left solely as a job for our Jewish neighbors. Victims of irresponsible hate, these children may now be helped by Christian love and concern."

Palestine Endowment Fund—photocopies of PEF Certificate of change of Number of Directors (1935) and Certificate of Incorporation (1922).

Szold, Henrietta, Reception Center Building Plans—architect's drawings (1947).

Constitution—numerous folders. The first contains copies of constitutions published in 1921, 1924, 1926, 1927, 1928, 1931, 1933, 1934 and 1941. Following this folder are to be found 4 folders (1921-1948) of memos, convention reports, correspondence (including chapters' suggestions), samples, etc., and 1 folder of photocopied material (largely duplicating that found in the above 4 folders) concerning changes in the constitution. In addition, 3 folders of correspondence and printed materials deal with chapter, regional, and Junior Hadassah constitutions.

(In drawer marked "HMO and Voc.")

First unlabeled folder—material of Hadassah Medical Relief Association including By-Laws (1923?), application for "Registration as a Foreign Company in Israel" (March 10, 1948), plus certificates of incorporation (June 4, 1925 and July 2, 1925).

Hadassah's Activities in Palestine—1923 and 1939 reports on Hadassah projects in Palestine.

Unlabeled folder following Medical Building Plans—correspondence related to the several editions of the Articles of Association of the HMO in Palestine (1921-1935).

HMO—Infant Welfare—reports and brochures concerning child welfare work (1923-1945), including work with infants, school luncheon programs and recreational facilities.

Medical School—a history of the Medical School from its inception (1936), including 4 agreements of affiliation (1936, 1940, n.d. and 1945) between Hadassah and Hebrew University to establish programs in graduate and undergraduate medical training and medical research. In a second folder are to be found architects' plans and photos of models of the Medical School buildings.

Hadassah Medical Organization—letter by "Zip Szold" (June 4, 1926) detailing the establishment of Joint Hospital Committee composed of representatives of Hadassah and the American Jewish Physicians' Committee for raising funds to establish a "series of hospital buildings of which the proposed Hebrew University shall be the cornerstone;" report (August 6, 1943) of Hadassah social service activities (Kupat Holim Amamit, medicine, school hygiene and infant welfare, soldiers' welfare and occupational therapy); income record of HMO 1918-1937; several printed items describing the work of HMO; and the legal papers establishing HMO as a corporation.

HMO—Health—numerous reports concerning health conditions and work of HMO (1917-1937).

HMO—Scientific Papers—2 folders containing research papers of HMO physicians.

HMO—Nathan Straus Health Center—correspondence and reports (1925-1928) concerning establishment of the Center, including the program of the cornerstone ceremonies; contains also photos, clippings, and further correspondence regarding the Center (1932 and 1946).

History–Szold, Henrietta, School of Nursing–numerous histories of the school and of nursing in Palestine and several brochures concerning the training program; cf. also the following folder labeled "H. Szold School of Nursing–Nurses" (Kaplan and Landy), which contains more of the above material, as well as files concerning the careers of Rose Kaplan and Rose Landy.

Vocational Education–a 62-page report on the role of vocational education in Palestine (1945).

Vocational Education–Seligsberg, Alice, and Seligsberg School– several biographies of A. Seligsberg, her correspondence, and reports on the school's activities.

(Files in the center of the room).

(In drawer marked "Palestine and Zionist Problems–Publicity")

History–Publicity Pamphlets–numerous publicity pamphlets, and reports detailing Hadassah's activities in Palestine (1918-1945).

History–Junior Hadassah–numerous publicity pamphlets, organizing manual and convention reports (1931-1948).

Unlabeled photo album–photos of various health facilities. History–Publicity concerning Rothschild Hebrew University Hospital Building Fund–numerous pamphlets, circulars, etc. (1935-1936).

History–Report of Survey of Organization and Administration– 1929 "Report of Survey of Organization and Administration Activities" of Hadassah and 1946 "Report of the Institutions of Hadassah . . . submitted to the Zionist Congress at Basel."

History–Testimonials–letters, clippings, etc. in praise of Hadassah's work (1926-1943).

History–Palestine and Zionist Problems–3 folders (1893-1948) containing a wealth of printed material, largely brochures and essays in various periodicals discussing a varied range of topics concerning Palestine, not specifically regarding Hadassah. Some of this material was issued by the British Government stating its position. Of special interest in folder #1 are an 1893 pamphlet published by the Friends of Zion entitled, "Jewish Colonization in Palestine. Its Origin, Causes, Condition, and Prospects"; and a reprint of A. Aaron Friedenwald's December 23, 1894 address delivered before the Mikveh Israel Association of Philadelphia, entitled "Lovers of Zion," published by the Zion Association of Baltimore (n.d.).

(In drawer marked "Articles–Youth Aliyah")

History—Misc. articles, reports and statistics—2 folders containing numerous annual reports, histories, articles, etc. concerning Palestine activities 1912-1948.

Hadassah History—Memoirs of Early Meetings—this folder contains a copy of the "Extracts from the Diaries of Mrs. Bernard A. Rosenblatt (Gertrude Goldsmith) of the years 1911, 1912, 1913, 1914, Relating to the Early Days of Hadassah Including Extracts from Minutes, Letters, etc. Mrs. Rosenblatt has all these minutes with her papers at home in Haifa, Palestine."

History—Misc.—items including a newspaper clipping (February 28, 1937), annual report for 1922, several histories of Hadassah, 1913 pamphlet in Yiddish discussing Hadassah's activities, original account sheets (3) (income and expenditures) of the "Palestine Account with Hadassah Chapter " (February 1, 1913-December 31, 1913), and the Treasurer's Report of the Daughters of Zion Hadassah Chapter (March 1, 1912-February 28, 1913). (For other dates cf. History—Financial Reports).

Chapter Instructions—Collated—"Hadassah Chapter Instructions Arranged Alphabetically under Activity, 1939-1941."

History—Founders of Hadassah—a listing of the original founders and a copy of the original invitation sent to organize Hadassah, which read: "The undersigned, in consultation with other women Zionists in New York City, have reached the conclusion that the time is ripe for a large organization of women Zionists, and they desire to invite you to attend a meeting for the purpose of discussing the feasibility of forming an organization which shall have for its purpose the promotion of Jewish institutions and enterprises in Palestine, and the fostering of Jewish ideals. The meeting will be held Saturday, February 24th, at eight P.M., in the Vestry Rooms of Temple Emanu-El, Fifth Ave. and 43 St."

History—Misc.—a 2nd folder with this label contains a listing of "Directors and Administrators of HMO" (1918-1928), a photocopy (original at Central Zionist Archives in Jerusalem) of the "Report of the Proceedings of the First Annual Convention of the Daughters of Zion of America held in Rochester, New York, June 29, and 30, 1914, at the Jewish Young Men's Association"; photocopy of a letter (March 3, 1912) from Bea Magnes discussing life in a totally Hebrew-speaking Jewish environment; blank certificates of Shekel Registration (1940); and various publicity materials.

History—Youth Aliyah—Meier Schfeyah—1926 report on the "endeavor to systematize the work at the Children's Village."

History—Youth Aliyah—Eddie Cantor and Misc.—news releases 1936-1938 concerning Eddie Cantor's Youth Aliyah activities and Youth Aliyah activities in general for this period.

Publications—"Malaria Control Demonstrations in Palestine" (HMO, 1922), and "Report of Dr. Israel Kliger and Medical Research Unit (Maintained by the American JDC in cooperation with the Government of Palestine). For Year Ending Aug. 31, 1923."
(In drawer labeled "Financial—Convention Reports")

Annual Reports—2 bound volumes of reports (1926-1932).

History—Financial Reports—financial reports (1912-1944).

History—Convention Programs—for most years 1924-1948.

History—Dr. Jesse Feinberg Material—material associated with the first AZMU, including Dr. Satenstein's passport (May 10, 1918), a large photo of the unit, musical programs attended, letter to H. Szold from the "Director" concerning the termination of Dr. Satenstein's stay in Palestine, etc.

History—Convention Reports—two-thirds of a file drawer of publications, including *Hadassah Yearbooks* (1935-1937), Convention Reports (1927-1931 and 1933) and educational materials.

Palestine and Zionist Problems—Balfour Declaration—historical retrospectives, material concerning celebration of Balfour Day (1942) and a typescript of an interview with H. Szold concerning Lord Balfour.

Palestine and Zionist Problems—minutes of Palestine Committee meetings (January 23, 1939-May 21, 1940).
(In drawer labeled "J. L. Magnes")

Dr. Magnes Letters—2 folders containing mimeographed copies of letters (1940-1943) to Mrs. David de Sola Pool concerning Hadassah's involvement with Hebrew University in cooperative health and medical education projects.

History—HMO Publications, Reports—various reports on HMO activities (1922-1924, 1933 and 1947-1948).

History—HMO—Straus Health Center—various reports (English and Hebrew) on the Center's activities (1930-1933 and 1936).

President's War Relief Control Board—5 folders (1939-1945) containing the request for permission from the U.S. State Department to undertake relief work in Palestine, reports and correspondence concerning the activities and copies of periodic reports to the State Department and War Relief Control Board.

HISTORY

(In same section as Permanent Files)

History—Membership—2 folders largely containing promotional materials and handbooks and membership statistics 1912-1948.

History—Membership Cards—sample cards for various years beginning 1922.

History—Medical Reference Board Reports—reports for 1942-1944.

History—Palestine Royal Commission Memorandum by Hadassah—3 copies of the "Memorandum Prepared by Hadassah . . . for the Palestine Royal Commission on American Interest in Medicine and Public Health Work in Palestine" (December, 1936); also the minutes of a Hadassah meeting concerned with Arab-Jewish Relations (March 11, 1943).

History—Publicity—3 folders of promotional materials, especially concerning JNF and Palestine Supplies Project.

Material not cataloged by repository.

Research access restricted. Photocopies not provided.

RM 5/75

2.   10 items, covering 1930s-1948 (stills from early 20th century), in Record Groups 885 B - 931 B.

In Israel Film Archives, Cinematheque, Jerusalem.

Collection includes 16-mm black and white film footage, shorts and newsreels dealing with all facets of Hadassah involvement in Israel; health and medical services, Youth Aliyah and education.

Of special interest are the following:

2a. "Hadassah 1940": silent film footage reused in later Hadassah Medical Organization documentary films. Subjects include Hadassah Hospital on Mount Scopus, 1939-1940 (nurses training program, emergency treatment, surgery and obstetrics wards); Youth Aliyah and Hadassah Children's Village; and shipments of medical and food supplies from the United States (Folder 916 B).

2b. "If I Forget Thee": the history of Hadassah Hospital on Mount Scopus; footage of the 1936 ground-breaking ceremony and Henrietta Szold; opening of the hospital in 1939; close of World War II; Arab terrorism and hospital under siege; plaques of U.S. donors (Folder 930 B, 931 B).

2c. "Henrietta Szold": 28-minute biography of Henrietta Szold filmed in 1947 (Folder 911 B; 928 B).

2d. "Forgotten Children": 10-minute film about Youth Aliyah, the child rescue movement sponsored by Hadassah, presented by the National Youth Aliyah Committee of Hadassah, narrated by Quentin Reynolds (Folder 892 B).

Collection cataloged by repository.

Research access not restricted. For use in institution only.

RA 5/82

HEBRA TARUMOT HAKODESH
(Founded in London in 1824 to provide funds for poor Jews in Palestine; American branch in existence, 1832-185?.)
18 items, covering years 1824-1857, in collection (I-33).
In American Jewish Historical Society, Waltham, Massachusetts.

Contains a printed copy of the proposal, dated 1824, from Solomon Herschell, the Chief Rabbi of England, to form the Hebra; manuscript letters in Hebrew and English, dated 1851 from Palestine, acknowledging receipt of funds from I. B. Kursheedt, Solomon Isaacs and Simon Abrahams of New York; Congregation Shearith Israel in Charleston, Nefutzoth Yehudah in New Orleans and the synagogue in Curaçao; and M. M. Nathan and James K. Gutheim of New Orleans; a printed copy of a letter from Hayyim Gagin (Sephardic Chief Rabbi in Palestine) to Zvi Hirschell requesting assistance; and an extract of the constitution and report of activities of the society published in New York in 1846.

Collection cataloged in repository.

Research access not restricted. Photocopies provided.

MF 9/74

HEBREW UNIVERSITY
2 boxes, covering years 1920-1935.
In Zionist Archives and Library, New York City.

Includes correspondence concerning contributions, book donations, fund raising, etc.; clippings from the American Jewish press; brochures promoting the establishment of a department of law and other programs at the Hebrew University; and photocopies of the minutes of the American members of the Board of Governors of the Hebrew University (May 12 and 13, 1934; June 26 and July 17, 1935) dealing with financial, operational and educational questions. Correspondents include Judah L. Magnes and Felix Warburg.
Material not cataloged by repository.
Research access not restricted. Photocopies provided.

RM 4/75

HERTZ, JOSEPH HERMAN, 1872-1946
(Born in Slovakia; moved to New York at age of 12; rabbi in Johannesburg, South Africa, 1898-1913; early Zionist and cofounder of the South African Zionist Federation; Chief Rabbi of the British Commonwealth, 1913-1946.)
1 item, dated 1934, in Record Group A354.
In Central Zionist Archives, Jerusalem.
The item is a 24-page report of the Conference of Governors of the Hebrew University residing in America, held May 12-13, 1934; the section on income lists American contributors, including among others the Jewish Teachers Association, the American Jewish Physicians' Committee, the Rockefeller Foundation, the American Friends of the Hebrew University, the Jacob and Theresa Schiff Memorial, the Joint Distribution Committee and Senator Arthur Vandenberg. Among the participants at the conference were Julian Mack, Cyrus Adler, Irving Lehman, Roger Straus, Felix Warburg, Stephen S. Wise, Louis Ginzberg and David Bressler.
Collection cataloged by repository.
Research access not restricted. Photocopies provided.

SH 5/81

HISTORY OF THE YISHUV
Ca. 680 items, covering 1847-1940s, in Record Group 4.
In Yad Ben Zvi Archives, Jerusalem.

Collection contains correspondence, record books, pamphlets and other documents relating to financial support of the Old *Yishuv* by American Jewry. Most of the material is in Hebrew, with some in Yiddish and English. The material pertains to:

Kollel America: correspondence, questionnaires and a record book (*pinkas*) (Folders 4/2/1; 4/2/2/12; 4/2/2/67; 4/2/6/30; 4/3/3-5; 4/3/6/4; 4/3/3/1-29);

Activities of messengers (*shadarim*) to America in the middle and end of the 19th and early 20th century: correspondence, letters of authorization and a legal document (Folders 4/1/2; 4/2/1/21; 4/2/2-3); and

Contributions of Americans to Eretz Yisrael, in part during World War I, as recorded in correspondence and record books. Much of the material relates to Bikur Holim Hospital, Etz Hayyim Yeshiva, Ezrat Nashim Hospital and Kollel Habad (Folders 4/1/1/14; 4/2/1; 4/2/1/24; 4/2/2-4; 4/2/7/5,13; 4/2/7/13; 4/3/6/3; 4/3/24; 4/3/18/5).

Of special interest are the following:

Ca. 233 letters of recommendation from ca. 1906 through the 1940s, written to Kollel America in Jerusalem on behalf of immigrants to Eretz Yisrael testifying to their eligibility for acceptance into the Kollel. Most are from the New York office of the Kollel, but several came from other American cities, including Denver, Pittsburgh and Philadelphia (Folders 4/2/1; 4/3/3-5), as well as from the leaders of the Safed community regarding the reinstatement of Yehudah Glazshtein to the lists of Kollel America (Folder 4/3/3/52);

Ca. 365 printed questionnaires from the 1920s and 1930s distributed to recipients of funds from Kollel America to determine the extent of their need. Data includes names of family members, date and place of birth, number of years spent in the United States, date of immigration to Eretz Yisrael and occupation (Folder 4/3/3/1-29);

"Memorial Book of the Mishna Study Society at Tifereth Yerushalayim Synagogue of Kollel America" (64 handwritten, bound folio pages in Hebrew), record book of the Society dedicated to daily Mishna study composed of Kollel America members. It contains the Constitution, list of members (95 men, 89 wives) and lists of officers of the Society; includes entries from 1905, when the Society was founded, until 1921; refers to a dispute between the Society and the Tifereth Yerushalayim Beit Midrash and a £50 donation by Jacob Schiff to the Kollel (Folder 4/2/1/20); and

2 letters (3 pages in all) written July 10, 1892 from messenger Jacob Moshe Broudo to Zalman Hayyim Rivlin involving an early attempt to import *etrogim* from Eretz Yisrael to America. 50 *etrogim* ordered by Rabbi Hayyim Ya'acove Widrewitz for Philadelphia (Folder 4/2/3/24).

Computerized index to 4/2/1-5 only. Remainder of collection classified but not cataloged.

Research access not restricted. Photocopies provided.

AF 2/82

IDELOVITCH, DAVID

15 items, covering years 1917-1918, in special folder in Record Group A192.

In Central Zionist Archives, Jerusalem.

Folder 227/13I contains the correspondence of the Special Committee for the Relief of Jews in Palestine, located in Alexandria, Egypt during World War I. Of special interest is a telegram from American Consul in Alexandria Garrels to Secretary of State Robert Lansing, Washington, D.C. (December 17, 1917) about relief for Palestine being held up in Alexandria.

Material cataloged by repository.

Research access not restricted. Photocopies provided.

TzB 2/75

INDUSTRIAL REMOVAL OFFICE

18 items, covering years 1904-1918, in collection (I -91).

In American Jewish Historical Society, Waltham, Massachusetts.

The collection consists of letters sent by the Federation of American Zionists (1904-1913) recommending people to the IRO for relocation (Box 22), as well as correspondence (1918) with the Provisional Executive Committee for General Zionist Affairs regarding "M. Yeshourun," a former resident of Palestine who wanted to live under conditions somewhat analogous to those of

Palestine and who was placed on a Corona, California plantation (Box 26).
Material cataloged by repository.
Research access not restricted. Photocopies provided.

JDS 6/75

ISAACS, MYER SAMUEL, 1841-1904
(Born in New York City; judge and teacher at New York University Law School; helped father, Samuel Myer Isaacs, establish Board of Delegates of American Israelites.)
5 items, in French, dated 1879-1880, in folder marked "Correspondence–Alliance Israélite Universelle" in collection (P-22).
In American Jewish Historical Society, Waltham, Massachusetts.
The correspondence relates to the activities of the Alliance Israélite Universelle on behalf of Jews in Palestine.
Collection cataloged by repository.
Research access not restricted. Photocopies provided.

MF 8/74

JEWISH AGENCY, AGRICULTURAL SETTLEMENT DEPARTMENT, JERUSALEM
(The department responsible for initiating and aiding Jewish agricultural settlement in Eretz Yisrael.)
4 items, covering years 1923-1924, interspersed in Folder 216a in Record Group S15.
In Central Zionist Archives, Jerusalem.
The items are correspondence with Nathan Straus and consist of a copy of a letter (January 18, 1924) from Frederick Kisch of the Palestine Zionist Executive requesting that Straus thank Mr. Rockefeller for work done by the Malaria Survey, funds of which were provided by the Rockefeller Foundation; and a Hebrew memo (December 27, 1923), Hebrew letter (January 4, 1924) and its English translation from Avraham Hartzfeld and A. M. Koler to Straus, outlining the need for modern dairies with pasteurization equipment and requesting his aid for their establishment.
Collection cataloged by repository.
Research access not restricted. Photocopies provided.

OZ 12/75

JEWISH AGENCY, POLITICAL DEPARTMENT, JERUSALEM, 1921-1948

(The department of the Jewish Agency—until 1929, the Palestine Zionist Executive—which dealt directly with the government of Palestine.)

Ca. 150 items, covering years 1923-1942, interspersed and in separate folders in Record Group S25.

In Central Zionist Archives, Jerusalem.

The collection contains documents and correspondence concerning the raising of funds and donations in the United States toward the upkeep of institutions in Eretz Yisrael. Folders 357, 704 and 1218 deal with donations by Nathan Straus; Folder 704 contains correspondence about the expression of appreciation to John D. Rockefeller for founding and funding the Malaria Survey; Folder 658 concerns the Masonic Palestine Foundation, which raised money for educational institutions in Eretz Yisrael; and Folders 642 and 7471 contain material on the Erlanger Farm Scholarships. Other American philanthropic activities on behalf of the *Yishuv* are found in Folders 357, 700, 3944-3946, 6093 and 6806.

Collection cataloged by repository.

Research access not restricted. Photocopies provided.

OZ 5/76

JEWISH INSTITUTE FOR THE BLIND, JERUSALEM

Ca. 150 items, covering years 1907-1939, interspersed in Record Group M17 (Temporary Boxes 406/1-4 and 408/9-11).

In Jerusalem Municipality-Historical Archives, Jerusalem.

The collection contains correspondence from the United States concerning contributions to the Institute. Of special interest is a letter from the American Embassy in Constantinople (August 3, 1915), signed by H. Morgenthau, about forwarding a contribution to the Institute through Consul Otis Glazebrook.

Material not cataloged by repository.

Research access not restricted. Photocopies provided.

RB 11/74

JEWISH NATIONAL FUND

5 boxes, covering years 1937-1948.

In Zionist Archives and Library, New York City.
   Contains confidential minutes, circular letters and pamphlets concerning the programs of the JNF.
Material not cataloged by repository.
Research access not restricted. Photocopies provided.

RM 6/73

JOSEPH, DOV (BERNARD), 1899-1981
(Born in Canada; settled in Jerusalem in 1921 after serving in the Jewish Legion during World War I; legal adviser then member of Jewish Agency Executive.)
5 items, covering years 1925, 1926 and 1941, in Record Group 5/4.
In Yad Yitzhak Ben Zvi, Jerusalem.
   The items consist of a 1926 pamphlet describing the work of the Histadrut Nashim Ivriot and listing Mrs. Robert D. Kesselman as president of the Jerusalem Playground Committee organized and administered by the Guggenheimer-Hadassah Recreation Committee (Folder 5/4/2/21); Americans on the Board of Trustees of the Young Judaea Scout Fund in 1925 (Folder 5/4/2/15); and a newspaper interview with Chief Rabbi Isaac Herzog concerning his trip to America in 1941 to raise funds to transport European yeshiva students to Eretz Yisrael (Folder 5/4/1/10).
Collection cataloged by repository.
Research access not restricted. Photocopies provided.

AF 4/82

KALLEN, HORACE M., 1882-1974
(Internationally prominent American-Jewish philosopher and educator.)
8 folders, covering years 1920-1948.
In YIVO Institute for Jewish Research, New York City.
   The collection contains material relating to the American Friends of the Hebrew University (including a letter from Felix Warburg [1925] inviting Kallen to become a member of the American Advisory Committee of the Hebrew University); the Julian W. Mack School and Workshops ("to provide young Jewish

children in Palestine . . . with elementary and industrial training"); the American Palestine Fund, Inc. (later the American Fund for Palestine Institutions, including minutes of Board of Directors January 14, 1941, August 12, 1942, July 31, 1944 and November 22, 1944, president's and treasurer's reports for 1940 and 1941; budget for 1944); the Friends of Bezalel; the New York Committee for Musical Instruments for Palestine; the American Palestine Music Association (Mailamm); the Palestine Endowment Fund; the Palestine Economic Corporation; the Palestine Exhibit at the New York World's Fair, 1939; and the Palestine Craft Education Society, organized 1939 "for the support of the Julian W. Mack School and Workshops in Palestine."
Bibliographic description published by repository.
Research access not restricted. Photocopies provided.

RM 11/75

KANN, JACOBUS H., 1872-1944

(Dutch banker and Zionist; founder of Zionist Organization in Holland and one of founders of Jewish Colonial Trust.)
Ca. 175 items, covering years 1923-1926, interspersed in Record Group A121.
In Central Zionist Archives, Jerusalem.

The two major subjects covered in the Kann file are the attempt to erect a library building in Jerusalem and to assist the Anglo-Palestine Bank. Of special interest is a letter to Julius Simon (February 15, 1926) about the great importance of the Anglo-Palestine Bank to Jewish settlement in Palestine (Folder 161/II). Also of interest is a letter to Rabbi Abraham Simon (October 1, 1923) about the library project (Folder 161/I.).
Material cataloged by repository.
Research access not restricted. Photocopies provided.

TzB 12/74

KEREN HAYESOD (PALESTINE FOUNDATION FUND)

(Financial arm of the World Zionist Organization, established in London in 1920.)
1.   18 boxes, covering years 1921-1950.

In Zionist Archives and Library, New York City.

Contains the Act of Incorporation and By-Laws, minutes of the Board of Directors (January, 1922-January, 1923; November, 1936; December, 1938; November, 1940; February-June, 1941; January-September, 1942; November, 1944; December, 1945; May, 1946; and June, 1947), minutes of the Finance and Economic Committee (January, 1941-September, 1942; January-December, 1944; and April 1946-June, 1947), in part concerned with the Economic Bureau Financial Reports, and minutes of the Administrative Committee (December, 1924-December, 1927; December, 1936-December, 1940; January, 1941-May, 1941; December, 1941; September, 1942; January, 1944-December, 1944; and May, 1945-April, 1947). Matters discussed include the Women's Keren Hayesod League Bazaar to raise funds to aid in "Women's Welfare Work in Palestine" (1926), UPA fund raising, JNF requests, Hebrew University Medical Department requests, reports on local conditions throughout the United States, the relationship between Keren Hayesod and Hadassah, the agreement between Keren Hayesod and the JNF, appropriations to the German Council in Palestine, Palestine exhibits in the United States and the Latin American Department's activities.

Includes also various financial reports (1921-1922, 1935-1940) concerning fund-raising projects and loans to Palestine organizations, Auditor's Reports (May, 1921-December, 1926 and May, 1947), Income & Expenditure reports (January, 1937-December, 1937 and January, 1939-December, 1939) and "UPA Comparative Data 1937-1938" concerning pledges and payments listed by community. Also contains material on financial transactions with regard to emigration, purchases of handicrafts made by the Bezalel Museum, and donation ledgers (April, 1921-June, 1923 and July-October, 1940); Keren Hayesod activities in America; the Palestine Economic Bureau's efforts to inform Americans on the economic situation in Palestine, including trade possibilities, and their exhibits at Radio City; and the Youth Department's "News in Brief" concerning fund raising and *Aliyah*. There is also a report on the first 25 years' activities of Keren Hayesod in Palestine, addresses by Louis Lipsky, Abba Hillel Silver and Bernard A. Rosenblatt, various broad-

sides and pamphlets, press releases (1947-1948) and material from the local groups of New York City, Brownsville and East New York, Westchester and New England.   Correspondents include Kurt Blumenfeld, Georg Landauer and Louis Lipsky.
Material not cataloged by repository.
Research access not restricted.   Photocopies provided.

RM 3/73

2.   1 box, covering years 1921-1928, in Jewish National Fund Papers.
In YIVO Institute for Jewish Research, New York City.

Contains the minutes of the Board of Directors (June, 1923 and October, 1925) concerning fund raising and appropriations to the Governing Board of the Hadassah Medical Organization, a report of the Committee on Keren Hayesod Statutes (1921), a report on the financial status of the Keren Hayesod (March, 1923), the minutes of a meeting of the Temporary Executive Committee of Keren Hayesod (August, 1921) regarding a tentative plan of reorganization, a memo on the legal status of the Keren Hayesod, organizing materials for local committees, clippings on Keren Hayesod activities in Buffalo and Dayton and correspondence to and from Emanuel Neumann and William Edlin.
Material not cataloged by repository.
Research access not restricted.   Photocopies provided.

RM 3/73

KLEIN, DAVID, 1880-1969
(Professor of English, College of the City of New York; secretary of the American Committee on the Library of the Hebrew University of Jerusalem of the ZOA)
1 folder, covering years 1918-1922.
In Zionist Archives and Library, New York City.

Includes correspondence, circulars and other material from Jacob De Haas, Henrietta Szold, Hugo Bergmann, Heinrich Loewe and organizations such as the ZOA, the Intercollegiate Zionist Association, the American Committee on the Library of the Hebrew University of Jerusalem of the ZOA, the Society of Physicians and

Dentists Interested in Medical and Health Problems of Palestine and the Library of Congress, concerning collecting books for the Hebrew University Library and for the Bibliothek "Shaar-Zion" of Jaffa.

Printed materials include a promotional brochure; a Land Certificate Agreement; Constitution of the American Zion Commonwealth; a report by Harry Fischel to the Palestine Development Council (October 21, 1923); and pamphlets and articles pertaining to this project in the *Maccabaean* and *The New Palestine*.
Material not cataloged by repository.
Research access not restricted. Photocopies provided.

RM 1/75

KOLLEL AMERICA TIFERETH YERUSHALAYIM
(Founded in 1896 by American Jews resident in Jerusalem; the constitution adopted by the American office in 1897 states as its purpose: "To aid and assist indigent and needy American Jews and Jews of other countries resident in Jerusalem and Palestine.")
1 item, covering years 1924-1947.
In Yad Yitzhak Ben Zvi, Jerusalem.

Item is 2 files, ca. 2 inches thick, containing applications of recipients of *Halukah* from 1924-1947.
Material not cataloged by repository.
Research access not restricted. Photocopies provided.

OZ 6/76

LEIBOVITZ, ZE'EV
1 item, in Record Group A65.
In Central Zionist Archives, Jerusalem.

Folder 6 contains the minutes of a meeting of the Joint Distribution Committee in Palestine concerning the distribution of funds to an orphanage. The minutes are written in Hebrew, on JDC stationery and are dated 3 Adar 5670 (1910).
Material cataloged by repository.
Research access not restricted. Photocopies provided.

TzB 11/74

LEVANON (BELLINKY) FAMILY
(Jerusalem family of Judge Mordechai Levanon who was born in Russia in 1888; served in Istanbul as correspondent for a New York Jewish newspaper and later settled in Israel and was president of the Yeshurun Organization in Jerusalem.)
5 items, covering years 1931-1941, in Record Group 5/12.
In Yad Yitzhak Ben Zvi, Jerusalem.

The collection contains correspondence and reports, some in Hebrew, relating to the role of the United Synagogue of America in establishing the Yeshurun Organization in Jerusalem; financial assistance extended by the United Synagogue and its affiliated Women's League; formation of a joint council of the United Synagogue and Yeshurun Organization; involvement of Henrietta Szold as liaison between the two organizations; and the transfer of Yeshurun property to the Keren Kayemet (Folders 5/12/3,11).
Collection classified by repository.
Research access not restricted. Photocopies provided.

AF 4/82

LEVIN, SHEMARYA, 1867-1935
(Born in White Russia; moved to Berlin in 1906 and settled in Palestine in 1924; prominent Zionist speaker and author; visited the United States several times, in part to solicit support for the Dvir Publishing Company, of which he was a founder.)
1 item, dated 1926, in private papers of Shemarya Levin (A20).
In Central Zionist Archives, Jerusalem.

Item is a memorandum (July 6, 1926) from Hadassah about health work in Palestine being carried out by the Hadassah Medical Organization and includes financial statements (Folder 63).
Collection cataloged by repository.
Research access not restricted. Photocopies provided.

SS 7/74

LEWIN-EPSTEIN, ELIAHU ZEEV, 1863-1932
(Arrived in the United States in 1900 and established Carmel Wine Company; went to Palestine in 1918 as member of American Zionist Medical Unit; settled permanently in Palestine where he

served as member of the Zionist Commission in 1919; returned to the United States on behalf of Bezalel and other Jewish interests.) Ca. 35 items, covering years 1915-1927, interspersed and in special folders in Record Group A216.
In Central Zionist Archives, Jerusalem.
      The collection contains ca. 30 letters (1915-1916) concerning sums of money to be paid to various charitable institutions in Palestine as well as to private individuals. The money was sent through the Provisional Zionist Committee and had previously been handled by the Carmel Wine Co. (Folder 6).
      Folder 36 contains correspondence (November 6, 1925 and April 29, 1926) about HIAS and whether it should help immigrants in Palestine. Of interest is a letter (April 3, 1927) from the Paris office of HIAS, describing the difficult economic conditions in Palestine causing a high rate of emigration. Rather than encourage immigration, help should be given to immigrants already in Palestine. The folder also contains two memoranda from the Provisional Executive Committee for General Zionist Affairs (January, 1915) on the condition of the Jewish wine growers in Palestine and on the proposed loan to the Jewish orange growers of Palestine. Included are lists of contributions for these loans.
Material cataloged by repository.
Research access not restricted. Photocopies provided.

OZ 12/74

LOEWE, HEINRICH, 1867-1950
(German Zionist and librarian.)
5 items, covering years 1922-1927, interspersed in Folder 42 of Record Group A146.
In Central Zionist Archives, Jerusalem.
      The main subject covered in this file is the library in Jerusalem and how money could be raised to support it. Of special interest is a letter from Aaron Ember to Professor Loewe (October 31, 1923), suggesting New York as a good place for fund raising.
Material cataloged by repository.
Research access not restricted. Photocopies provided.

TzB 1/75

MACK, JULIAN WILLIAM, 1866-1943
(U.S. judge; prominent Jewish communal figure and Zionist leader; a founder of American Jewish Committee; president of American Jewish Congress, 1918; president of Zionist Organization of America, 1918; Israeli settlement Ramat ha-Shofet named in his memory.)
1 linear foot, covering years 1913-1939.
In Zionist Archives and Library, New York City.

The collection begins with a large folder of material removed from various files for the purpose of writing a biography. Included in this folder is material depicting Mack's participation in soliciting contributions for the Deborah Kallen school and for the Yemenite Children's Home in Rehovot and the Palestine Endowment Funds.

Among the extensive material from the Palestine Endowment Funds are accountants' reports (1931 and 1932); a report of the "Jewish Organizations in Palestine Serving the Jewish Population, 1927"; a financial statement of the S. Marcus Fechheimer Trust Fund of the PEF (September 30, 1928); correspondence of the Hebrew Secondary School (Beth Sefer Reali Ivri) and of the School of the Parents Educational Association (Deborah Kallen), including financial statements for 1926-1928; an agreement between Henry Friend and F. H. Kisch, Albert Hyamson, A. Goldwater and Harry Sacher to establish a trust for the Jewish Blind Institute (January 24, 1925); and correspondence (1926-1939) with Judah Magnes, Robert Szold, Stephen Wise, Emanuel Mohl, Vladimir Jabotinsky, Albert Einstein and Chaim Weizmann, regarding the Hebrew University (including bank statements of the Hebrew University Building Fund, 1930-1933), the endowment of the Institute of Jewish Studies, the Dead Sea Concession (Palestine Chemicals, Ltd. and Palestine Potash, Ltd.) and the Palestine Musical Art Foundation (including also its certificate of incorporation, budget for 1937-1938, and memos and the correspondence of the American Palestine Music Foundation.)

Other matters covered in this collection are the funding and activities of the Jewish Institute of Technology (1913-1915), the establishment of the Ben-Yehuda Memorial Association and fund raising by Ben Yehuda's widow for the posthumous publication of his dictionary and correspondence between Mack and the various

organizations in Palestine to which he made contributions (the American Committee for the Jewish Blind Institute of Jerusalem, the Bezalel Art School, the Palestine Immigrant Welfare Committee, and Haifa Technical Institute, the Palestine Orphans Committee of America, the Jewish National Fund and the Hebrew University). Material cataloged by repository.
Research access not restricted. Photocopies provided.

RM 1/75

MANDATORY GOVERNMENT, CHIEF SECRETARY'S OFFICE (1918-1925)
2 items, dated 1923, in Folder 146 in Record Group 2.
In Israel State Archives, Jerusalem.

The items contain information regarding contributions to the University of Jerusalem: $10,000 contribution by Felix Warburg, described as a "known opponent of Zionism" but sympathetic to the work done in Eretz Yisrael, and an announcement by Zionist leader Morris Rothenberg of a promise by the Committee of American Jewish Physicians to provide $10,000 for the installation of a Roentgen laboratory.
Collection cataloged by repository. Published catalog available.
Research access not restricted. Photocopies provided.

TG 4/81

MANDATORY GOVERNMENT, DEPARTMENT OF ANTIQUITIES, PALESTINE ARCHAEOLOGICAL MUSEUM
Ca. 105 items, covering years 1927-1948, in Record Group ATQ 202.
In Archaeological (Rockefeller) Museum, Jerusalem.

The collection includes correspondence, lists of invitees, reports, architectural plans and other material chronologically arranged, documenting the American role in the construction and maintenance of the Palestine Archaeological (Rockefeller) Museum and its programs; the $2 million contribution by John D. Rockefeller, Jr.; proposal for the museum; Rockefeller's pledge of funds for construction in correspondence with the High Commissioner, Herbert O. Plumer, and James H. Breasted of the Oriental Institute of the University of Chicago; laying of foundation stone; proposed staff and organization of the Department of Antiquities with special reference to conditions arising from the Rockefeller contribution; progress and financial reports on construction; and the opening of the museum to the public in 1938.

Of special interest are the following:

copy of a letter (October 13, 1927) from John D. Rockefeller, Jr. to High Commissioner Plumer pledging up to $2 million toward the cost of building, equipping and endowing the Museum proposed to Professor James H. Breasted. (Jacket 1);

a 4-page handwritten proposal entitled *Proposed Palestine Museum* (November 7, 1927) by E. J. Richmond, Director of Antiquities, to Plumer stating guidelines for proceeding with construction by the Government of Palestine of an archaeological museum; suggesting that procedures be adopted in which "the confidence of the authorities in America be retained"; strongly recommending Austin St. B. Harrison to be the architect. (Jacket 1);

a 3-page letter (November 18, 1927) to the secretary of state for the colonies, informing his superior of plans for procedures in construction of the museum and reasons for selecting Harrison as architect. Mention is made of Harrison possessing the confidence of Breasted, to whose initiative the Rockefeller gift was due and who keeps Rockefeller informed of progress in the work. Harrison in cooperation with Breasted prepared preliminary plans for the Museum (Jacket 1);

"List of invitations issued by Department of Antiquities for the laying of the Foundation Stone of the New Museum" (ceremony held June 19, 1930). Among the invitees were Dr. and Mrs. C. C. McCown, Dr. W. F. Albright, Dr. C. S. Fisher and Jacob Spafford, Esq. (Jacket 1);

a 4-page "List of invitations sent out for an informal inspection of the Palestine Archaeological Museum—11.1.38." Among the invitees were the director, American School of Oriental Research (Nelson Glueck) and Mrs. Glueck; Professor S. V. McCasland (ASOR) and Mrs. McCasland; Dr. C. S. Fisher; Mr. Gordon Loud; the president, Hebrew University (Judah Magnes) and Mrs. Magnes; and American Consul-General Wadsworth and Mrs. Wadsworth.

Two jackets of collection are cataloged; several boxes of uncataloged material.

Research access not restricted. Photocopies provided.

RA 5/82

MANDATORY GOVERNMENT, DEPARTMENT OF EDUCATION

14 items, covering years 1923, 1925, 1938 and 1942-1948, in Record Group 8.

In Israel State Archives, Jerusalem.

The collection contains letters, memos, pamphlets and reports concerning the contributions by American Jewish individuals and organizations to various educational institutions such as: Hebrew University (Folders 1031/1236/61, 1058/2996/1/PE); Agudat Israel schools (1041/1626/51); Yeshivat Merkaz HaRav (1037/ 1386/60); Gymnasia Herzlia (1028/1174/66); Gymnasia Ivrit (1026/1134/58); and Etz Hayyim Yeshiva and Talmud Torah (1045/ 1757/52).

Collection cataloged by repository.

Research access not restricted. Photocopies provided.

HK/DP 3/82

MANDATORY GOVERNMENT, DEPARTMENT OF MIGRATION (1920-1948)

Ca. 25 items, covering years 1925-1932, in Record Group 11.

In Israel State Archives, Jerusalem.

The collection contains correspondence, reports and press extracts regarding contributions from the United States to various educational institutions in Eretz Yisrael, including Yeshivat Merkaz HaRav, Jerusalem (Folder 1171/8); Yeshiva of Lomza, Petach Tikva (Folder 1171/17); and Gymnasia Herzlia, Tel Aviv (Folder 1171/15), as well as individual rabbis supported by Kollelim from American funds (Folder 1172/18). Statements on contributions were submitted to the Immigration Department to show the financial stability required in order to obtain immigration certificates.

Besides reports of organized World Zionist fund raising, the material mentions contributions, loans and endowments by various American Jewish leaders such as Mrs. Felix Warburg, Nathan Straus,

Samuel Untermyer and Samuel Lamport (Folder 1223/20).
Collection cataloged by repository.
Research access not restricted. Photocopies provided.

HK 1/82

MASLIANSKY, ZVI HIRSCH, 1856-1943.
(Born in Byelorussia; active in Hibbat Zion movement; immigrated
to United States in 1895; eloquent and influential Yiddish orator
who popularized Zionism among Yiddish-speaking immigrants to
the United States.)
2 items, dated 1925, in Record Group V. 1282.
In Jewish National and University Library, Jerusalem.
    The items are correspondence from Rabbi Yaacov Harlap
seeking the assistance of Masliansky and the Adath Pinsk community
in New York in arranging a monthly stipend for three refugee
families from Pinsk settling in Eretz Yisrael (File 94).
Collection cataloged by repository.
Research access not restricted. Photocopies provided.

SK 3/82

MATERIAL FOR PALESTINE
1 item, undated.
In Zionist Archives and Library, New York City.
    Item is a press release announcing a shipment of noncontra-
band items to Palestine.
Material not cataloged by repository.
Research access not restricted. Photocopies provided.

RM 6/73

NAMIER, LEWIS BERNSTEIN, 1888-1960
(Born near Warsaw; served in the British army in World War I and
subsequently in various departments of the British Foreign Office;
professor of history at Manchester University; political secretary
of the Jewish Agency, 1929-1931 and political advisor, 1938-1945.)
1 item, dated 1947, in Record Group A312.
In Central Zionist Archives, Jerusalem.
    Item is a letter reporting a decision by the American Friends
of the Technion to raise half a million dollars for the Technion to

erect electrical and chemical laboratories in a project headed by Albert Einstein, Chaim Weizmann and Frieda Warburg.
Collection cataloged by repository.
Research access not restricted. Photocopies provided.

SH 6/81

NEAR EAST RELIEF
(Interreligious relief association.)
4 items, covering years 1922-1924, interspersed in collection (M-1562).
In the Archdiocese of Boston Archives, Brighton, Massachusetts.
    Consists of correspondence dealing mainly with allegations of anti-Catholicism against the organization.
Collection not cataloged by repository.
Research access not restricted. Photocopies provided.

JDS 7/78

NORTH AMERICAN RELIEF SOCIETY FOR THE INDIGENT JEWS IN JERUSALEM, PALESTINE
(Established in 1853; still in existence in 1948.)
1.   16 items and one account book, covering years 1853-1887, in collection (I-14).
In American Jewish Historical Society, Waltham, Massachusetts.
    Contains a copy of the certificate of incorporation (1853), financial records and correspondence addressed chiefly to the treasurer, Myer S. Isaacs, from Sampson Simpson (1857), Moses Montefiore (1858) and Louis Loewe (1887) and several letters from Jerusalem pertaining to receipt of and requests for funds.
Collection cataloged by repository.
Research access not restricted. Photocopies provided.

MF 8/74

2.   1 box, covering years 1853-1947.
In American Jewish Archives, Cincinnati, Ohio.
    Contains a copy of the Articles of Incorporation (February 14, 1853), in which the purpose of the Society is stated as being "to establish a permanent fund, the interest of which shall be annually applied to the relief of Indigent Jews in Jerusalem, Palestine."

Includes also the minutes and treasurer's reports for the years 1908-1947, which are concerned mostly with the amounts of funds distributed and the organizations to which these donations were made.
Material not cataloged by repository.
Research access not restricted. Photocopies provided.

RM 6/73

PALESTINE COMMITTEE OF THE NATIONAL ASSOCIATION OF JEWISH CENTER WORKERS
1 item, dated 1938.
In Zionist Archives and Library, New York City.

Contains a report submitted at the annual convention in Washington, D.C. (May 25-31, 1938) regarding implementing a program on Palestine and Zionism in the Jewish Community Center.
Material not cataloged by repository.
Research access not restricted. Photocopies provided.

RM 6/73

PALESTINE EMERGENCY FUND
4 items, undated.
In Zionist Archives and Library, New York City.

Contains material concerning the fund-raising matches in Madison Square Garden, New York City.
Material not cataloged by repository.
Research access not restricted. Photocopies provided.

RM 6/73

PALESTINE ORCHESTRA FUND, AMERICAN COMMITTEE
1 folder, covering years 1936-1940.
In American Jewish Archives, Cincinnati, Ohio.

Contains correspondence relating to contributions, the purchase of sheet music (1 list included), and relief work carried on by the Orchestra in hiring refugees from Germany and Austria (1938).
Material not cataloged by repository.
Research access not restricted. Photocopies provided.

RM 6/73

PALESTINE RESTORATION FUND, GREATER NEW YORK CAMPAIGN COMMITTEE

(Established 1918 by the World Zionist Organization to provide funds for its budget; liquidated in 1918 and funds transferred to Keren Hayesod.)

1 item, dated 1918.

In YIVO Institute for Jewish Research, New York City.

Item is a circular letter announcing a benefit for the raising of money to aid Jewish settlement in Palestine.

Material not cataloged by repository.

Research access not restricted. Photocopies provided.

RM 2/73

PALESTINE STATEHOOD COMMITTEE

(5 committees related to Revisionist wing of Zionism; Hillel Kook (Peter Bergson) and Eri Jabotinsky were among its important leaders.)

Ca. 100 items, covering years 1939-1949, interspersed in collection. In Historical Manuscripts, Sterling Library, Yale University, New Haven, Connecticut.

Contains material dealing with efforts to raise funds for the 5 committees, as well as conflicts with the Zionist Organization over contributions and correspondence with the Internal Revenue Service regarding tax exempt status.

Collection cataloged by repository.

Research access not restricted. Photocopies provided.

JDS 2/75

PEOPLE'S RELIEF COMMITTEE

(Established August, 1915, representing labor element of American Jewish community, to collect funds for Jewish war sufferers in Europe; in November, 1915 became one of three separate commissions of Joint Distribution Committee.)

Ca. 100 items, covering years 1920-1924, interspersed in collection (I-13).

In American Jewish Historical Society, Waltham, Massachusetts.

Consists primarily of correspondence in English, Hebrew and Yiddish between B. Zuckerman, general manager of the People's

Relief Committee, and the officials of the Histadrut Kellalit and Palestine Workman's Fund regarding the dispersal of committee loans, donations, books and clothes to various needy Jewish cultural and philanthropic institutions in Palestine in the post-World War I period. The bulk of the correspondence is with Ephraim Blumenfeld (David Bloch), David Ben-Gurion and Yitzhak Ben-Zvi. Of particular interest is the refusal of the Workmen's Fund to distribute free clothes to members who considered it immoral to receive free goods for which they were still able to pay.

Collection cataloged by repository.

Research access not restricted. Photocopies provided.

JDS 6/75

PHI EPSILON PI
(Jewish college fraternity established in 1904).
Ca. 38 items, covering years 1925-1948, in Boxes 16-17a of collection (I-76).
In American Jewish Historical society, Waltham, Massachusetts.

Consists of correspondence dealing with Phi Epsilon Pi's financial support of the Hebrew University (1925-1948), the Jewish Agricultural Orphanage of Palestine (1937), the Jewish National Fund (1936-1937) and the United Palestine Appeal (1937).

Collection cataloged by repository.

Research access not restricted. Photocopies provided.

JDS 6/75

PIONEER WOMEN
(Founded 1925 as American Labor Zionist women's organization.)
2 boxes, covering years 1936-1948.
In Zionist Archives and Library, New York City.

Includes material concerning festival programs, development of the women's labor movement in Palestine, various New York and national conventions with reports delivered on these occasions (1938-1939, 1942-1946 and 1948), the work of and fund raising for Moetzet Hapoaloth Children's Homes, lectures on "The Background of Socialist Zionism" and "Moses Hess," study groups, Child Rescue Fund, Revisionists, Mishkei Poaloth, monthly program materials, the struggle for Independence, Beth Zeiroth Mizrachi,

Baleka Settlement Homes, the Kanot Youth Village and Agricultural School, Omna (home for orphans and children of widowed mothers), the Ein Karem Youth Village and the Girl's Sewing School.

Contains also financial statements for 1936-1939, 1942-1945 and 1947-1948 and *News of the Month* and *News and Views*.
Material not cataloged by repository.
Research access not restricted. Photocopies provided.

RM 1/75

RADLER-FELDMAN, YEHOSHUA, 1880-1957
(Born in Zborov, Galicia; Hebrew journalist and teacher; arrived in Palestine in 1907; a founding member of Berit Shalom association advocating a binational state for Arabs and Jews; wrote under pen name Rabbi Binyamin.)
Ca. 19 letters, covering years 1945-1948, in Record Group A357.
In Central Zionist Archives, Jerusalem.

Collection includes correspondence between Rabbi Binyamin and Rabbi Meir Kovner regarding Rabbi Binyamin's intervention with the Norman Scholarship and Fund to ensure American financial support for Porat Joseph Yeshiva in Rehovot and sending an emissary to the United States, and between Rabbi Binyamin and Rabbi Moshe Zvi Neriah regarding the New York Joint Distribution Committee support for Kfar Haroeh Yeshiva (Folder 88).
Collection cataloged by repository.
Research access not restricted. Photocopies provided.

SG 12/81

ROKACH, ISAAC, 1894-1974
(Active in business affairs connected with the citrus industry in Palestine; director of the Pardess Syndicate of Palestine Citrus Growers, 1927; editor of *Hadar*, citrus monthly.)
4 items, covering years 1932, 1946-1947, in Record Group A323.
In Central Zionist Archives, Jerusalem.

The items consist of a letter regarding placement of an agricultural student from Eretz Yisrael at a Michigan college (Folder 120/3); a mimeographed report (in Hebrew) for 1946 of B'nai B'rith activities, which included a monthly publication mailed to the United

States to familiarize American Jewry with B'nai B'rith projects in Eretz Yisrael, e.g., assisting in the absorption of immigrants and initiating a campaign to build a youth center (120/3); and correspondence concerning the Palestine Art Exhibition in America sponsored by the World Jewish Congress (127/2).

Folder 64 contains an unusual letter in Hebrew, dated 1932, from the Cincinnati, Ohio B'nai B'rith Lodge, asking for financial aid from Rokach and explaining that local funding had stopped and it devolved upon Palestine Jewry to support the lodge while the U.S. economy was in such deep depression.

Collection cataloged by repository.

Research access not restricted. Photocopies provided.

SG 11/81

RUPPIN, ARTHUR, 1876-1943
(Father of Zionist settlement in Eretz Yisrael; b. Germany; settled in Eretz Yisrael before World War I; economist and sociologist.)
3 items, dated 1922, in Folder 258 in Record Group S55.
In Central Zionist Archives, Jerusalem.

The items consist of correspondence between Arthur Ruppin and Louis Lipsky regarding past and future donations to the Hebrew University by Solomon Rosenbloom and efforts by Shaare Zedek Hospital to elicit donations from America.

Collection cataloged by repository.

Research access not restricted. Photocopies provided.

DF 11/81

SAFED
Ca. 13 items, covering years 1898-1921, in Record Group 4° 1263.
In Jewish National and University Library, Jerusalem.

The collection includes lists of donors and letters in Hebrew and Yiddish regarding financial contributions from America and their distribution among the Jews of Safed. Letterheads attest to numerous landsmannschaften in America formed to help Jews from the same country or town who went to Eretz Yisrael.

6 items deal with the relationship between Roumanian Jewish immigrants to America and Kollel Roumania; the Central Committee

of Roumania in America; the First Roumanian-American Congregation; the Convention Committee of Pittsburgh Zion Societies (Tiphereth Zion Society, Daughters of Zion, Dorshie [sic] Zion Society and Shoshanas Zion Society); the United Galil Aid Society (founders and supporters of the General Orphan Asylum, Public Kitchen at Safed and Immigrant Sheltering Home at Haifa) and the Kehillat Sha'arei Shamayim (community of Roumanian immigrants to America) (File 11).

Small contributions for the poor in Safed (1928-1929) are enclosed in letters from Rabbi Pinchas David Halevi Horowitz of Boston and Abraham Albert and Pinchas Margaliot of the United Galil Aid Society in New York to Mrs. Miriam Segal, wife of a rabbi in Safed (File 63). The distribution of *haluka* in Safed is discussed in a letter (1897) to Rabbi Yehuda Segal from the "Trustees of Charity for Jerusalem of New York" (File 61). An invitation (29 Adar 5679-1919) to the Kollel Hasepharadim to participate in the allocation of funds received from New York is located in File 4F.

Collection cataloged by repository.

Research access not restricted. Photocopies provided.

SK 5/82

SALANT, SHMUEL, 1816-1909
(Born near Bialystok, Russia; arrived in Jerusalem 1841; Ashkenazi Chief Rabbi of Jerusalem from 1878 until his death.)
79 items, covering years 1891-1899, in Record Group 4$^{\rm O}$ 1359.
In Jewish National and University Library, Jerusalem.

The collection includes private correspondence with enclosed donations from America (Folders 1-2, 4, 6, 8, 11-12, 15-16, 18, 20-28, 32-33, 39-40 and 58) and reports from emissaries, including lists of donors and amounts contributed by each (41-44 and 46-51).

A poignant example is an undated letter in Hebrew from Rabbi Solomon I. Scheinfield of Louisville, Kentucky, bearing a $25 donation, saved cent-by-cent by a poor elderly man for an old people's home in Eretz Yisrael, with the request that residents of the home say kaddish annually on the yahrzeit (Folder 34).

Material in the collection is in Hebrew, Yiddish, English and German and includes references to Hebron Yeshiva, Bikkur Holim Hospital and B'nai B'rith.
Collection cataloged by repository.
Research access not restricted. Photocopies provided.

SK 4/82

SAN FRANCISCO, CONGREGATION SHERITH ISRAEL
1.   5 items, covering years 1868-1872, interspersed in collection (I-97).
In American Jewish Historical Society, Waltham, Massachusetts.
The items are 4 letters from Moses Montefiore to D. Meyer, president of Congregation Sherith Israel in San Francisco, thanking him for his congregation's contributions to Jewish charities in Palestine, and 1 receipt from the Jewish authorities in Jerusalem to Montefiore for the 1872 contribution that Montefiore personally delivered.
Collection cataloged by repository.
Research access not restricted. Photocopies provided.

JDS 6/75

2.   1 item, dated 1876.
In American Jewish Archives, Cincinnati, Ohio.
Contains a letter from Moses Montefiore to B. Scheideman, Esq., thanking the congregation for their donation of £10 for the needy in Jerusalem.
Material not cataloged by repository.
Research access not restricted. Photocopies provided.

RM 6/73

SCHWARZ, LEO W., 1906-1967
(American author and editor.)
2 boxes, covering years 1946-1948.
In Zionist Archives and Library, New York City.

Contains material concerning the establishment and activities of the Hebrew University Committee of America under ZOA sponsorship, whose purpose was to assist in financial matters and also "to interpret the program of the Hebrew University to the American public and to establish rapport with the American academic world." Contains also a substantial amount of material from the American Friends of the Hebrew University and on the Hebrew University itself.

Includes also the manuscripts of N. Bentwich's biography of J. L. Magnes and fragments of the autobiography of Irma Lindheim not included in the published version, mostly dealing with her early life in America and her becoming a Zionist during World War I. Correspondents include I. S. Wechsler, Leon Simon and Leon Roth.

Material not cataloged by repository.

Research access not restricted. Photocopies provided.

RM 1/75

SEGAL, MOSHE ZVI, 1878-1968

(Born in Lithuania; rabbi in Great Britain until settling in Eretz Yisrael in 1926; taught Bible at the Hebrew University until 1949.)

2 items, dated 1931, in Record Group 4° 1183.

In Jewish National and University Library, Jerusalem.

The items are letters from Julian Morgenstern of the Hebrew Union College, Cincinnati and David de Sola Pool of the Spanish and Portuguese Synagogue, New York discussing financial assistance for publication of scholarly works by Segal (File 4).

Collection cataloged by repository.

Research access not restricted. Photocopies provided.

SK 3/82

SIRKIS, DANIEL, 1882-1965

(Born in Poland; settled in Eretz Yisrael, 1925; headed Jewish Council in Tel Aviv-Jaffa.)

2 items, dated 1929, in Record Group A340.

In Central Zionist Archives, Jerusalem.

The items consist of correspondence between Meir Bar-Ilan, in New York at the time, and Sirkis on the subject of fund raising in the United States for religious institutions in Eretz Yisrael (Folder 14).
Collection cataloged by repository.
Research access not restricted. Photocopies provided.

DF 11/81

SOCIETY OF JEWISH PHYSICIANS AND DENTISTS
INTERESTED IN THE MEDICAL AND HEALTH PROBLEMS
OF PALESTINE
5 items, dated 1920-1922.
In Zionist Archives and Library, New York City.

Contains correspondence concerning the establishing of a chapter in Boston (original chapter in Chicago) and a forthcoming meeting at which it was hoped that Albert Einstein would be in attendance.
Material not cataloged by repository.
Research access not restricted. Photocopies provided.

RM 6/73

SOLIS-COHEN, SOLOMON, 1857-1948
(American Jewish physician and poet; active in communal affairs; non-Zionist member of the Jewish Agency.)
Ca. 10 items, covering years 1930-1941, interspersed in collection (P-30).
In American Jewish Historical Society, Waltham, Massachusetts.

In Folder marked "Hebrew University" there are 8 items of correspondence, dated 1930-1934, with various individuals including Marcus A. Rothschild of the American Jewish Physicians' Committee, concerning the campaign to erect a medical school at the Hebrew University. In Folder marked "Correspondence Relating to Palestine", there is correspondence with Julian Mack, dated 1941, concerning funds for the United Palestine Appeal.
Collection cataloged by repository.
Research access not restricted. Photocopies provided.

MF 8/74

SZOLD, HENRIETTA, 1860-1945
(Born in Baltimore; active in Jewish and Zionist organizations; founding leader of Hadassah, went to Palestine in 1920 as interim director of the American Zionist Medical Unit and remained until her death, except for frequent visits to the United States; held positions in the Jewish Agency Executive, the Vaad Leumi, and Youth Aliyah.)
1.   1 item, dated 1917.
In American Jewish Archives, Cincinnati, Ohio.

Item is a letter to Mrs. Kameretzsky of the Youngstown, Ohio, Hadassah Chapter regarding fund raising for relief work in Jerusalem undertaken by Hadassah.
Material not cataloged by repository.
Research access not restricted. Photocopies provided.

RM 6/73

2.   Ca. 600 items, covering years 1920-1945, interspersed and in special folders in Record Group A125.
In Central Zionist Archives, Jerusalem.

The material in this collection can be divided into several major areas. Material relating to work done with girl juvenile delinquents in Palestine is found in Folder 40. Boy juvenile delinquents are discussed in letters found in Folder 118. Model kitchens for the teaching of cooking are described in Folders 115 and 116.

Work on behalf of Youth Aliyah is described in Folders 94, 95, 96, 101, 103, 104 and 105. The activities of Hadassah for Palestine and miscellaneous items are described in Folders 9, 22, 23, 106, 110 and N10/13. Material relating to the nutrition fund is found in Folders 53 and 70; clothing distribution in Folder 50; soup kitchens in Folders 38, 39 and 41; and plans for a girls' home in Folder 68.
Material cataloged by repository.
Research access not restricted. Photocopies provided.

TzB 11/74

SZOLD, HENRIETTA (THE JEWISH AGENCY, OFFICES OF THE MEMBERS OF THE EXECUTIVE, 1928-1930)
Ca. 35 items, covering years 1927-1929, interspersed and in special folders in Record Group S48.
In Central Zionist Archives, Jerusalem.

The collection contains correspondence about major financial contributions to Hadassah and other Zionist causes (Folders 2, 4, 15 and 41). Of interest in Folder 2 is a letter from E. Deinard of New Orleans to H. Szold (dated Adar Sheni, 1929) donating his property in Ramle to Hadassah.

Folder 4 contains correspondence about a $100,000 contribution by Nathan Straus and a $30,000 contribution by Carl Fechheimer of the Pittsburgh Fund.
Material cataloged by repository.
Research access not restricted. Photocopies provided.

OZ 11/75

UNITED BREZINER RELIEF COMMITTEE
(Committee established in 1945 from representatives of Breziner Landsmanshaften in New York, Chicago and Los Angeles to assist Breziner throughout the world.)
1 item, dated 1945, in Folder "Jewish Agency" in Box 3 of Judge Jonah L. Goldstein Collection (P-61).
In American Jewish Historical Society, Waltham, Massachusetts.

Contains a memorandum concerning the activities of the United Breziner Relief Committee on behalf of Breziner refugees in Palestine.
Material cataloged by repository.
Research access not restricted. Photocopies provided.

MF 10/74

THE UNITED HOME FOR THE AGED IN JERUSALEM
(Established in 1878 as The House for the Aged.)
8 registers (books), covering years 5687-5694 (1927-1934), in Record Group 2078-1.

In Jerusalem Municipality–Historical Archives, Jerusalem.

The book consists of lists of contributors and contributions to the Home, mostly from the United States.

Material not cataloged by repository.

Research access not restricted. Photocopies provided.

RB 9/74

UNITED JEWISH APPEAL

4 boxes, covering years 1934-1948.

In Zionist Archives and Library, New York City.

The collection contains the following material relating to the aid of the Jews in Palestine: confidential reports of the Allotment Committee (1940, 1941 and 1943); minutes of the Executive Committee (February 13-March 11, 1935 and October 18, 1935); minutes of a meeting to discuss war chests (July 10, 1942); financial reports (1934, 1935, 1940 and 1943); campaign manuals (1935, 1939, 1940, 1943, 1946 and 1948) and other promotional materials; correspondence concerning Keren Hayesod's fund-raising activities for 1934 and UJA fund raising for 1939; printed pamphlets and reports (including *Security for German Jews In Palestine, The Emigration of German Jewish Children and Youth to Palestine*, by Leo Baeck (1935), *The Fighting Jew in Palestine*, and a Supplement to *The Needs of Palestine*); speeches, National Conference Programs (1945-1946); and press releases.

Material not cataloged by repository.

Research access not restricted. Photocopies provided.

RM 1/75

UNITED PALESTINE APPEAL

(Established in 1925.)

1.   10 boxes, covering years 1926-1948, interspersed in collection.

In Zionist Archives and Library, New York City.

Contains the certificate of incorporation of the UPA (May 20, 1927), established "to voluntarily aid, encourage and promote the development of Jewish life in Palestine." Also contains the minutes of the Administrative Committee (October, 1926-October, 1927,

March-November, 1937, December, 1938, May 1941 and April, 1942); of the Negotiating Committee of the JDC and the UPA (December, 1939 and October, 1940); of the Finance Committee (October, 1926-October, 1927); of the Executive Committee (October, 1926-October, 1927, June, 1944, November, 1944, October, 1947 and March-April, 1948); of the Budget Committee (March, 1944); of the Board of Directors (October, 1926-October, 1927, December, 1947 and February, 1948); and of special conferences held in March and June, 1927. Also includes the reports of the National Emergency Conference of 1933, of the Annual Conference of 1938 and of the National Conference for Palestine of 1940; statistical and descriptive financial reports of income and expenditures for 1926-1929, 1931-1944 and 1948 (some confidential) of the UJA by the UPA and numerous printed materials for circulation and publicity.

Materials that explain the program of the UPA include "1937 Campaign Quotes for U.P.A.," "Questions and Answers about the U.P.A." (1937), "Some Notes on the Budget of the 12,000,000 Dollar War Emergency Campaign of the U.P.A." (1939), "Palestine— Key to Jewish Immigration Needs and the German-Jewish Problem" (1939), "The Jewish Settlements in Palestine at the End of the Year 5700" (1940), "Jewish Immigration into Palestine and its Financial Requirements" (1941), "1942 Budget for War-Time Aid to Upbuilding of Jewish Homeland," "U.P.A.: An Appraisal" (1942) and "A Statement to the 1943 Allotment Committee."

Includes memos and correspondence dealing mainly with internal administrative matters, conditions in Europe and the *Yishuv*, and with the raising and distribution of funds. Includes also numerous speeches by Abba Hillel Silver, Stephen S. Wise, Chaim Weizmann, Nahum Goldmann, Bernard Rosenblatt and other prominent persons in Zionist affairs; press releases (1937-1948); and materials from the East Side Eretz Yisrael Conference of the UPA (1926). Correspondents include Julian Mack, Stephen S. Wise, Morris Rothenberg, Henry Montor and Abba Hillel Silver.
Material not cataloged by repository.
Research access not restricted. Photocopies provided.

RM 1/75

2.   1 item, dating from 1940s, in Record Group 565B.
In Israel Film Archives, Cinematheque, Jerusalem.

Item is a 20-minute, 16-mm color film entitled "A Day in Degania," photographed by Lasar Dunner, edited and narrated by Maurice Samuel, describing "a day in a Palestine Colony typical of the hundreds established with American funds to provide security and freedom for harassed and homeless Jews."
Collection not cataloged.
Research access not restricted. For use in institution only.

RA 5/82

UNITED ZIONISTS-REVISIONISTS OF AMERICA
(Created in 1925 for the establishment of a democratic Jewish State with a Jewish majority on both sides of the Jordan.)
1 folder, covering years 1947-1948.
In Zionist Archives and Library, New York City.

Contains the *Newsletter*, broadsides and position papers and material on the Tel Hai fund-raising effort and the Jabotinsky anniversary celebration.
Material not cataloged by repository.
Research access not restricted. Photocopies provided.

RM 6/73

USSISCHKIN, MENAHEM, 1863-1941
(Born in Russia, active in Hovevei Zion and in World Zionist Organization; settled in Palestine in 1919 as member of the Zionist Commission and Palestine Zionist Executive; chairman of the executive council of the Jewish National Fund, 1923-1941.)
2 items, dated 1926, interspersed in Folder XVII, in Record Group A24.
In Central Zionist Archives, Jerusalem.

Both items are letters in Hebrew from David Yellin in New York to Ussischkin about the Teacher's Seminary in Jerusalem. One, dated 10 Tammuz, 5686, concerns obtaining funds for the school from Julius Rosenwald and others; the other, dated 2 Elul, 5686, is about obtaining teachers.

Material cataloged by repository.
Research access not restricted. Photocopies provided.

TzB 11/74

WIDER MINISTRIES OF FRIENDS, UNITED MEETING RECORDS

Ca. 50 items, covering years 1923-1948.
In Friends United Meeting, Wider Ministries Commission, Richmond, Indiana.

Consists of scattered letters dealing with efforts to collect money for the American Friends Mission in Ramallah, Palestine, founded by Eli Jones in 1867. A large portion of the letters are in the papers of Khalil and Eva Rae Totah and Mildred E. White. Collection cataloged by repository.
Research access not restricted. Photocopies provided from microfilm.

JDS 11/78

WISE, STEPHEN SAMUEL, 1874-1949

(Internationally prominent American rabbi, communal figure and Zionist leader.)
Ca. 1000 items, covering years 1912-1948, interspersed in collection (P-134).
In American Jewish Historical Society, Waltham, Massachusetts.

The collection contains correspondence and other materials relating to the appeals, politics and philanthropic activities of the following Palestine-related charitable organizations in which Wise was active: Hadassah (1915-1948) (Box 100-7, 8); the Palestine Foundation Fund (1924-1948) (Box 102-1); the 1915 Palestine Relief Fund, which was greatly aided by Nathan Straus (Box 102-2); the United Palestine Campaign, United Jewish Appeal/United Palestine Appeal, and the Allied Jewish Campaign (1924-1948) (Boxes 101-4, 126-2, 129-13 and 130-2), the files of which also contain minutes, budgets, reports, brochures and circular letters; the American Friends of the Hebrew University (1921-1948) (Boxes 126-3 and 127-3); the American Fund for Palestinian Institutions (1943-1948) (Box 126-4); the Jewish National Fund (1926-1948)

(Box 128-5, 11); the Men's League for Palestine (1935) (Box 128-17); the Palestine Hebrew Culture Fund (1938-1945) (Box 129-6); the Near East Relief Organization (1914-1944) (Box 128-20); the Palestine Lighthouse, Inc., the charitable arm of the Jewish Blind Institute (1929-1947) (Box 129-9); and the American Relief Society for the Yemenite Jews of Jerusalem, Palestine, Inc.(1928-1937) (Box 130-4).

The files "Charities in Palestine 1924-1940" (Box 126-9), "Orphan Problem 1918-1919" (Box 129-2) and the miscellaneous correspondence (Box 130-14, 15) include references to other assorted charities with which Wise corresponded.

Philanthropic activities are also mentioned in Wise's correspondence with the following individuals: L. Baktansky (Box 104-7); Bernard Baruch (Box 104-9); Meyer Berlin (Box 104-12); Louis Brandeis (Box 106-3, 6 especially); Jacob De Haas (Box 107-22, 24); A. H. Fromenson (Box 109-18); Solomon Goldman (Box 110-1); Richard Gottheil (Boxes 110-6 and 111-2); Horace Kallen (Box 112-2); Benjamin G. Leve (Box 113-8); Irma Lindheim (Box 113-13); Henry Morgenthau (Box 116-14, 17); David de Sola Pool (Box 118-10); Samuel Rosensohn (Box 119-2); Arthur Ruppin (Box 119-7); Benjamin Selling (Box 119-15); Abba Hillel Silver (Box 119-20); Nathan Straus (Box 120-6, 7); Henrietta Szold (Box 120-11, 12); Robert Szold (Boxes 120-13 and 121-2); Chaim Weizmann (Box 122-1,4); Jessie Sampter (Box 130-5); and Maja Rosenberg (Box 130-6).

Wise also entitled aid for the Beth Sefer Reali (Box 126-8); the Zebulun Palestine Seafaring Society (Box 130-5); the Bezalel Art Museum (Box 130-7); and Mailamm—the Palestine Institute of Musical Sciences (Box 130-14).

Of special interest are the 12-page 1913 report of the National Conference of Jewish Charities, Committee on Palestinian Charities describing the successes and failures of the group set up in 1912 to organize and regulate Palestinian charities and "to be representative of all the branches of the religious community and to be authorized and encouraged to receive benefactions designed for Palestine and to distribute these in accordance with its own discretion" (Boxes 126-9 and 110-6); the several hundred items relating

to the attempt by Prof. David Yellin to collect money for his Jerusalem Hebrew Teachers College (1913-1938), which reveal the frustrations and difficulties then faced by needy Palestinian institutions in their dealings with Americans (Box 127-1,2); the correspondence dealing with the history of the Rosenbloom $500,000 donation to the Hebrew University, the plans for its use, their cancellation and the eventual substitution of a $100,000 building gift (1926-1934) (Box 127-4, 5); and the correspondence and documents relating to the Bertha Guggenheim Palestine Playground Fund (1927-1932) detailing the building of playgrounds in Jerusalem and other cities by the fund's American trustees (Stephen S. Wise, Irma Lindheim and Julian Mack) (Boxes 129-10 and 100-7).
Collection cataloged by repository.
Research access not restricted. Photocopies provided.

JDS 6/75

ZIMRO
(Musical group organized in Russia about 1918.)
1 scrapbook and 1 box, covering years 1918-1920.
In Zionist Archives and Library, New York City.

Contains correspondence from the ZOA concerning its proposed assistance, both financial and managerial, in the work of "ZIMRO" (Palestine Chamber Music Ensemble) on tour in America and on their way from Russia to Palestine: "1—To give concerts of Hebrew Music. 2—To collect Funds, the profits of which are to go towards a Zionist Fund. 3—To organize an association on which shall be represented Jewish musicians from all parts of the world. 4—To establish a Temple of Arts in Palestine." Includes also letters of introduction and recommendation from other Zionist organizations in Russia, the Dutch Indies, Shanghai and Palestine, attesting to their musical and fund-raising abilities; and advertisements, posters, programs, photographs and clippings from the English and Yiddish press about their tour throughout the major cities of the United States and abroad.

Material not cataloged by repository.
Research access not restricted. Photocopies provided.

RM1/75

ZIONIST ORGANIZATION, THE JEWISH AGENCY FOR PALESTINE, CENTRAL OFFICE, LONDON.
(The Central Office moved to London from Berlin after the 1920 London Conference.)
Ca. 30 items, covering years 1918 and 1933-1939, interspersed in Record Group Z4.
In Central Zionist Archives, Jerusalem.

Relevant items consist mainly of correspondence and documents concerning the Hadassah Women's Organization efforts to raise money for Palestine, especially for a medical school at the Hebrew University (Folder 17089). Folder 17296 contains some correspondence about a $100,000 donation made by B'nai B'rith in 1936. Folder 1593 includes 2 copies of a letter (July 7, 1918) from Louis D. Brandeis to Nahum Sokolow, in which the former is transmitting funds, collected by American Jews in honor of his 60th birthday, to the foundation of the Hebrew University.
Collection cataloged by repository.
Research access not restricted. Photocopies provided.

OZ 8/75

ZIONIST ORGANIZATION OF AMERICA
(American Organization of General Zionists; formed in 1918 by a merger of the Federation of American Zionists and other American Zionist groups.)
9 folders, covering years 1926-1948.
In Zionist Archives and Library, New York City.

The collection contains material on the Chicago exhibition of the Bezalel School of Arts and Crafts of Jerusalem (1926); confidential minutes of the meetings of the American Economic Committee for Palestine (1933); a report on the Palestine Pavilion at the New York World's Fair (1939); a copy of *Inside Palestine* volume I, number 2, concerned with the future of American-owned orange groves in Palestine (1941); a confidential report of a meeting with Senator Owen Brewster of Maine by Abba Hillel Silver and Elihu Stone on the relationship of American oil companies to the future of the Jewish National Homeland (1944); and reports and associated material of the Palestine Economic Bureau (1946-1948). Material not cataloged by repository.

Research access not restricted. Photocopies provided.

RM 3/73

ZLOCISTI, THEODOR, 1874-1943
(Physician and early German Zionist; member of city council of Tel Aviv.)
3 items, undated, in Folder 57 of Record Group A48.
In Central Zionist Archives, Jerusalem.

The collection contains material pertaining to the Hebrew University, funds available to it and the organization of the American Jewish Physicians' Foundation for the establishment and support of the Medical Department of the Hebrew University in Jerusalem. Of special interest are the preliminary statutes of the latter organization.

Material cataloged by repository.
Research access not restricted. Photocopies provided.

TzB 1/75

Index

Palestine Investors Service, 51
Palestine Jewish Medical Association, 71
Palestine Land Development Company, 42, 51
Palestine Lighthouse, 62, 128
Palestine Milk Station Fund, 78
Palestine Mining Syndicate, 48
Palestine Musical Art Foundation, 107
Palestine Office, 42
Palestine Orchestra Fund, 113
Palestine Potash Works, 9-10, 40, 48-49, 107
Palestine Purchasing Service, 22
Palestine Relief Fund, 122
Palestine Savings and Investment Corporation of the Bronx, 42-43
Palestine Securities, 43
Palestine Tobacco Growers Association, 38
Palestine Water Company, 11
Palestine Workmen's Fund, 115
Palestine Young Agriculturalists Organization, 57
Palestine-Zion Investment Corporation, 27
Pan Am Airways, 33
Pardes Hanna Agricultural Secondary School, 70
Pardes Orange Growers Cooperative Society, 38
Pasteur Institute in Palestine, 61
Peel Commission, 39
People's Relief Committee, 43-44, 114-15
Pewsner, B., 51
Phi Epsilon Pi, 115

Pioneer Women, 115-16
Pool, David de Sola, 53, 120, 128
Pool, Tamar de Sola, 84, 92
Porat Joseph Yeshiva, Rehovot, 116
The Presbyterian, 72
Provisional Executive Committee for General Zionist Affairs, 106

Radler-Feldman, Yehoshua, 116
Red Mogen David, 60, 73, 86
Reynolds, Quentin, 94
Richards, Bernard Gerson, 26, 57
Richmond, E. J., 109
Rivlin, Zalman Hayyim, 97
Rockaways Palestine Corporation, 4
Rockefeller Foundation, 95, 98-99
Rockefeller, John D., 108-9
Rockefeller Museum, 108
Rogers, Starr, 49
Rokach, Isaac, 44, 80, 116-17
Roosevelt, Franklin Delano, 83
Rosenau, Milton, 13
Rosenberg, Maja, 128
Rosenblatt, Bernard A., 7-8, 43, 102, 125
Rosenblatt, Louis J., 43
Rosenbloom, Solomon, 117
Rosensohn, Samuel J., 47, 83, 86, 128
Rosensohn, Sol, 48
Rosental, T., 79
Rosenwald, Julius, 13, 126
Roth, Leon, 120
Rothenberg, Morris, 5, 46, 108, 125